AF897230

IT COULD HAPPEN TO ANY OF US

TYSHEEM CROCKER
CEO of S.G. PUBLISHING

IT COULD HAPPEN TO ANY OF US. Copyright@ 2022 by Tysheem Crocker. All rights reserved. No part of this book may be used or reproduced in any manner whatsoever without written consent except in the case of brief quotations embodied in the media and reviews. For information contact S.G. Publishing (929) 328.6016.

FIRST ADDITION

COVER DESIGN: S.G. PUBLISHING
ISBN: 978-0-9828144-8-2
WEBSITE: www. sgpubl.com

Dedicated to Omar Jennett & Naquan Crocker-Jennett.

The rocks to my roll...

Also by Tysheem Crocker
Under the pseudonym BOOG DENIRO:

RESPECT THE STRUGGLE
NO SELLOUTS
NOTHING IS SACRED
CAN'T STOP WON'T STOP
THE UNGODLY PASTOR
URBAN ROYALTY
RED RUBI

IT COULD HAPPEN TO ANY OF US

TYSHEEM CROCKER
CEO of S.G. PUBLISHING

Contents

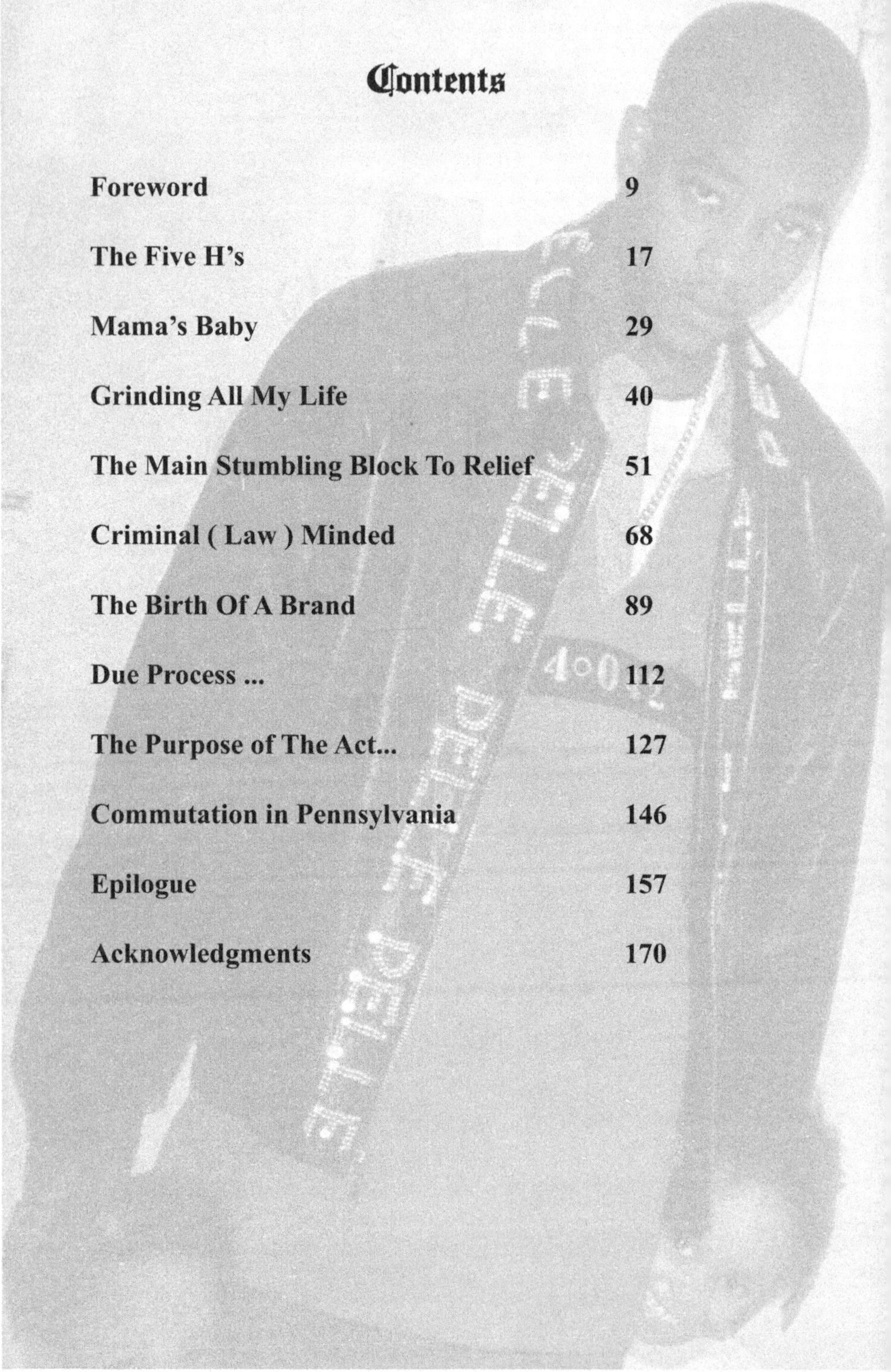

It is world knowledge that the wrongfully convicted stand at a great disadvantage when it comes to finding evidence and gathering new information, where excellent investigation is a necessity in order to uncover exculpatory evidence. Couple that obstacle with the TIMEBAR and a daredevil is born...

Foreword

As a kid, growing up in the Bronx, I thought I would become a legend for my accolades and accomplishments on the streets. Thought I would land in the pantheon of street scholars because I was getting to that bag. Never did it cross my mind that battling the criminal justice system would make my story legendary.

And what makes a legend? *Doing something very few have achieved.*

Let me make something very clear: *I have never accepted this as my fate*. I have never walked this walk without making complaints. Without being disgruntled. Without trying to do something about it. My efforts have amounted to many sleepless nights. My unrighteous attempts at righting this manifest wrong has landed me in the hole for long periods of time. I'd been met with great resistance by prosecutors. One had even lied on the stand, under oath, to keep me in prison. I was in prison throwing bricks at the prison not because I wanted to, but because I had no other choice.

It takes a special type of person to survive these types of droughts. You try to imagine waking up everyday without a purpose. *That's the life of a Lifer.*

Women left me, they thought I was finished. People stole

from me because they thought they would never have to face me again. I lost my mother to cancer.

Many would be unwilling to admit this, maybe even afraid, but here it goes! Several years existed where I was shrouded in humiliation, and super ashamed about my situation. Point blank being imprisoned for life (*especially for a crime I didn't commit*) left me unable at times to look in a mirror. Just the idea of being condemned, viewed as irredeemable, and side-eyed as *the walking dead* does something to the psyche and the esteem. So, for as long as I could, I hid my sentence while there existed people who weaponized the devastating blow.

I never hid my sentence out of deception, never had a desire to mislead anyone, I was only protecting my feelings and emotions from further injury. But in the process, I had inflicted pain. When the truth surfaced, chicks would be like, "*Ty, why didn't you just tell me? You could've told me!*" (*I'm telling you, the advancements of the world wide web is bananas. Anything can be Googled. Yes, even your case and the outcomes. And chicks be on it.*)

"*That's not something easy to discuss*," would be my natural response. And just like that, what took time building was destroyed in no time.

Sentences like this weren't just designed as deterrents to crime for those deserving, but also as invitations for further rejection, and reason to discount one's worth.

I lost everything when I came to prison.

Makes one wonder: is it better to have had it and lost it, or to never have had it at all????

See, when you had it, you know how to get it back...

"Congratulations, Mr. Crocker. You are now a Business Technology graduate..." the instructress had cheerfully announced, placing evidence of this accomplishment in my waiting and eager hands. After two and a half years of being educated by her six courses in total, I had finally completed the curriculum. While the streets had prepared me for the entrepreneurial world, now school had prepared me for the business world!!!

Prior to that day, fall of 2003, such a joyous and momentous feeling had eluded me. I had not graduated from elementary school, Jr. high school, or high school. And, I had never smiled harder.

Unfortunately for me, Accounting, Business English, Human Relations, Typing 1, Word, and Access/Excel would not have been on my radar had I not been incarcerated. Truth be told, I hated school when I was growing up in the Bronx. *Too many distractions.* School was secondary, while the streets were necessary.

And then ever so suddenly, knowledge had become the most important thing in my small and miniscule world. Academics and scholarly attributes were things I now coveted.

Those would become things I worked hard to acquire and attain that no one could ever take from me.

Education is what I relied on in my twenties, and into my thirties, almost in the same way an addict is dependent upon its drug of choice. During those years of incarceration, I completed Drug & Alcohol Education (12.5 hrs.), Thinking For A Change, Life Skills, Violence Prevention, and Breaking the Chains. Also, I have a certificate in Creative Writing, finishing at the top of my class in 2013.Though some of those classes/groups were prescriptive, it was my choice whether or not to participate. It was my choice whether or not to quit.

Through education, my cognitive thinking had been refined, my impulses had been curbed, my urges to indulge in drugs and liquor had been subdued, and my ability to build had never been more efficient. Academics were redefining my perception of reality, and magnifying my imagination.

However, this growth and development was no easy feat. Along the way I'd made many mistakes, several bad decisions, and did things I am not proud of. Sometimes circumstances dictate habit. And habits dictate behavior. One day I would feel like I had everything going for me, and then the next I would feel like I had nothing to live for. That is because, prison isn't about rehabilitation, it's about how much suffering can one take.

I was an all around good student, above satisfactory, but

once I left that education building I was venturing back into darkness. *And defiance seems to dance its best in the cloak of darkness.*

There were times I've felt helpless. Times I'd feel cheap, working for pennies when competent counsel cost tens of thousands of dollars, and productive Private Investigators carry hefty price tags. *Attorneys and PIs don't take Honey Buns and candy bars.* I felt like I was in this hell on earth all alone. Times existed when I felt like it had to be this way, because the only time my soul didn't ache is when I was accomplishing something.

I needed to be uncomfortable in order to ward off complacency. I needed struggle because that invites urgency. And everyday I wore that brown uniform or that brown sweat suit, it was a reminder of what I'd left behind, and what I needed to get back to. I was the bread winner in my family. I was securing the bag.

In addition to prison being uncomfortable, prisoners are also unable to go after the moments that will define who he or she is as a person. *We're just known as numbers.*

These institutions (*prisons*) were built to warehouse poor, uneducated people with propensities for violence, while institutions of higher learning were erected with exclusion in mind. The misconception is: *we're incapable of complying with the organizational expectations of western civilization.*

With that said, I think there are five ways in which to visualize prison. THE HANGOUT, THE HIDEOUT, THE HOTEL, THE HOSPITAL, THE HOSTAGE SITUATION. I call this philosophy *THE FIVE H's*...and I will be laying it out in the first chapter.

At the age of twenty-six, I made one of the best decisions of my life. I started writing my first novel. The process began with an intention and concluded with a commitment. Regardless of obstacles, or the length of time or the road ahead, I was on a mission.

By my 30th birthday, I had a business plan for S.G. Publishing. Today, I have penned double digit novels, published nine independently, met some of the culture's top writers along the journey, and entertained offers to make movies.

But, my greatest accomplishment is: I learned how to interpret American criminal law, and craft legal arguments. It proved to be a valuable skill, having been accused and convicted of conspiring to commit murder. Yes, I was forced to undertake such a tedious, meticulous and demanding path. People weren't lining up to help me. I was strapped for cash. I was undoubtedly at rock bottom. And I am innocent.

There is only a statute of limitation on Innocence if we allow for it. There is only an expiration date on justice if we allow it.

So, yes, education changed my perspective, while creative

writing saved my life. *Progress comes in pieces, my friends...*

IT COULD HAPPEN TO ANY OF US is not an autobiography. This is an inspirational and informational book including explosive interviews, anecdotes, criminal law, and the circumstances surrounding my wrongful conviction.

I've suffered from PTSD, I battled depression, I've represented myself in the court of law for many years, I've been denied a new trial a dozen times, I have exceeded expectations. I also continued to imagine. *Imagination is its own form of courage.* Each denial, dismissal, AFFIRMED, was a lesson learned about my case, and about the American criminal justice system. And that is: *No matter what we do, how far we have come, Blacks will always be looked at with great suspicion...*

Survival and attracting light in a place of utter darkness takes time and perseverance. I landed a Legal Dream Team by thinking outside this box.

In addition to telling this story of survival, I have interviewed three men on three very important topics: *DUE PROCESS, THE POST CONVICTION RELIEF ACT*, and *COMMUTATION IN PENNSYLVANIA*.

The good, the bad, the ugly, IT COULD HAPPEN TO ANY OF US...

This book was created with the ability to be read and digested in chronological order, or each chapter can be read individually.

"The imagination is sometimes more important than knowledge..."

—Albert Einstein, 1879-1955, physicist

Chapter One
The Five H's

The Five H's

The Hangout, The Hideout, The Hotel, The Hospital, The Hostage

In January of 1998, Rikers Island was gangland, the battlefield of a bloody war between two races, Blacks and Latinos, that lasted almost four years before a truce was agreed upon.

When I was dumped on Rikers, the backstory was front and center. I cannot front, I was fascinated by the gory details and the sudden unity the lifestyle had created. Through five principles, New York City's underworld had been unified! A city that once suffered from territorial unrest had a common goal: obliterate racial group oppression.

I'd been thrown into the lion's den, at a point in life where a male is no longer considered a boy, but not quite yet a man. Maybe a more befitting term than lion's den is: *THE DEVIL'S NEST*.

I credit that tumultuous time of captivity to my ability to exert the necessary power to prosper despite the limitations prison places on a kid. And that is a mentality very different than the one that can take you to the top on the streets. *Prison will swallow you whole, one large gulp, if you are not mentally fit.*

Six months of my life was spent in G.R.V.C.—0909 Hazen

Street—notoriously known as the Beacon. By several years, I was the youngest fugitive on 19-Block. Attempted murder, murder, and armed robbery were most of the charges on the rap sheets. Standing 5'7", just 140 lbs., it was there that I learned: *if I didn't continue making decisions for myself, like I'd been doing on the streets, somebody else would be making decisions for me...*

The universal consensus is: prison is a very dangerous place. And that it is. And every time I came out my cell, I had to be on point. Because it could pop at a moment's notice. Overall, though, the strong survive, but the powerful prevail.

There is an ecosystem in direct correlation with anomalistic ambition. Care, custody, and control is the motto of the Department of Corrections, but once I got that classification number, I was on my own.

It didn't hurt that I had a comrade by the name of Tankhead who had not only survived that Rikers Island gauntlet, but he also had a legendary name in the prison system. At the age of sixteen he had gone in, and by the time I hit Rikers, he was twenty-one and *O.G. had been added to Tankhead.* As young dudes, running the streets of New York, we'd had a few gains and losses together. Our neighborhood was brimming with violence.

If you're not strong or powerful, not connected to dudes who are, prison is horrible. With that said, there's nothing wrong with keeping a low profile. After all, it's about getting home, lavishing in liberties and the sensations of society. I don't know any dudes, (serious about legacy), who enjoy incarceration.

Now, I say this with absolutely no gratification—*The Beacon had become another hangout for me*. The allure was not just magnetic, pulling me in, but equally as intoxicating; in the same way street life had been to me eight years earlier.

Different baddies (*women*) pulling up on visits every other day, prime time phone slots (*8 PM - 10:45 PM*), and getting blunted everyday had put me at a great disadvantage. No question, getting back to my family, my cars, and my spot in the winning circle resided at the forefront of my young mind. But I wasn't doing anything to avoid this wrongful conviction.

As a result, I had no sense of direction. Just lawless principles predicated on survival—while 200 miles away, as an alleged gang leader, prosecutors in York County were lining me to take the fall for a 1997 murder case.

Prison politics had a stronghold on me. I was so consumed, so entrenched, I didn't even realize how bad things were getting for me. Although, I hadn't pulled the trigger, and I wasn't present when the murder went down, conspiracy laws was rearing its ugly head.

The day after Michael Jordan's Chicago Bulls won their sixth ring, my fugitive warrant was executed. And in York,

Pennsylvania, I had been formally charged with conspiracy to commit murder.

Though I was thoroughly prepared for whatever prison could throw my way, I was not prepared for what the York County Assistant District Attorney was planning... That's because I was hanging out. When I got to York County Prison the games didn't stop.

Exactly six months from June 15, 1998, (the day I was removed from New York and brought to PA), I was convicted of conspiracy to commit murder, and sentenced to LIFE in prison.

I thought I would come back on appeal after sitting for three, four, maybe five years, but here it is 2022 and I've served nearly a quarter century of unjust incarceration.

* * *

Because there were no outstanding men in my life when I was growing up is no excuse for how things turned out for me. I could've got out, I should've got out, but I didn't get out the game. Now I was in prison, hanging out. Want to know what that got me??? convicted of a crime I didn't commit.

Anything that could have gone wrong had gone wrong. Nothing about me said business. Nothing said I was taking this whole thing serious. And to think, *I was in the streets calling shots*.

The morning of jury selection, I got down to the receiving

room of York County Prison, where I learned that I would be going to trial in Foam Posits and a gray sweat suit. A friend of mine, Cindy Marion, had mailed my trial clothes overnight, but the mail room had rejected the UPS package because I had not taken the proper channels to have it accepted by the mailroom. A policy was in place addressing this very matter, but I didn't know anything about the mail room policy because I was in prison hanging out.

An all-white jury convicted a black boy dressed like he was going to a pickup basketball game, not just because the prosecution withheld exculpatory information, not just because his best friend framed him, but because he did nothing to prevent it.

It is so critical and incumbent upon us that upon detainment we hit the law library, that we understand the charges, that we reference the statutes and check the controlling law that the government intends to use to support their theory of the crime. It is imperative that we know the prison policies where we are being housed awaiting trial.

As a conscious Black man, treading the waters of injustice, my imagination will not allow me to cheat myself of the reality that those jurors handling my fate in 1999 thought, *look at this super predator! He didn't even have enough sense to wear a suit and shoes for trial...*

At the time of my apprehension, arrest and prosecution,

the terminology SUPER PREDATOR had just begun to resonate. It was associated with threat. *A domestic threat to societal norms*. It derived out of a necessity to curb the influx in crime, specifically in the inner cities of America. Young black men became targets as a result.

Prosecutors, judges, and all white juries put more Black people away during this era of tough-on-crime than any other time in American history.

First Lady, (*at the time*), Hillary Clinton was the first politician I ever heard use the term—*SUPER PREDATOR*.

It was the launch pad for then Senator Biden to introduce his legislation, which ultimately became known as *the 1994 Crime Bill* that disproportionately imprisoned minorities and made it extremely hard to fight a wrongful conviction.

I'm sure neither of these politicians saw this far into the future to witness just how destructive *the terminology* and *Bill* would be nearly 30 years later. They were just pandering to their base and constituency, I imagine. But I will never allow my imagination to overrule my common sense. Surely those jurors knew they had a duty and an opportunity to put away a SUPER PREDATOR, even if certain things didn't make sense.

I was left with regrets I live with everyday.

Proceeding to trial with a lawyer who wasn't with me.

Being ignorant when it came to the prison rules.

Being unaware that a constitutional protection was: I pick my jury.

And being unaware of what evidence was admissible and what was inadmissible.

Being wrongly convicted was an awakening for me. A rude awakening too. I had to accept the reality that my life was in shambles, and it would take a miracle to reverse this fate.

And for that, I'm witnessing seeds I'd planted many years ago sprout into beanstalks.

The man with no vision, unable to see past where he is in life, is no different than the man without a land. *He is lost.*

As we learned in this chapter, I was once lost. Which brings me to the purpose of this chapter ...

Everyone has their very own perception of reality. Everyone on lockdown copes with the pressures of prison differently. Though we own some of the same principles and even traits, we possess totally different perspectives. Quite frankly, prison is something different to everyone who is faced with the challenge.

I see it this way...

To some, *prison is a hangout.* When I first came to this devil's nest, I was one of them young dudes hanging out and putting no work in to protect my future.

To others, *it's a hideout.*

Some see prison *as a hotel.*

Then there's that few who see prison *as a hospital.* There is also a fraction of prison population who view prison as *a hostage situation.* When I look in the mirror, a hostage glares back at me.

This is just my philosophy, and I call it *the Five H's.* THE HANGOUT, THE HIDEOUT, THE HOTEL, THE HOSPITAL, THE HOSTAGE SITUATION.

Five H's is based on experience, as well as what I've had a front row seat to for over 24 years. And I'm going to break it down in hopes of enlightening those interested in self-awareness, self awakening, and eventual elevation.

Prison doesn't have to be—end all be all.

H-1) *The hangout!* That select sector of brothers too consumed with playing games instead of making the time count. Basically, (*and at times subconsciously*), they're approaching the prison experience like it's nothing serious, favoring insignificant occurrences over important matters.

Whether you're serving one or 100 years, nothing should be more important than regaining your freedom. If it's not going to be through the parole board, then it has to be through the courts. *Maybe even commutation.* But, don't cheat yourself by treating prison like it's a hangout.

H-2) *The hideout!* Now this is heavy. And I can't count how many times I saw it...

The sands of time have dwindled, it's time to roll, and a

dude does something dumb to go to solitary, fully aware that an automatic parole hit will follow.

Whenever there's an opportunity to reunite with love ones, that moment must be seized. And if you have to, then relocate and start over. But do not stay on prison grounds any longer than you have to. Because tomorrow is not promised.

H-3) *The hotel!* I understand it can be hard for some dudes to function in society, let alone thrive in the world, because of institutionalization, but languishing in prison is not the answer to that conundrum. Sadly, there is a portion of dudes who actually live better in prison than they do on the streets. So, they keep coming back, or outstay their welcome. The government calls it recidivism, I call it "*life on an installment plan.*"

H-4) *The hospital!* There exists a select case of people who commit crime because healthcare is almost free in prison. Maybe if healthcare was affordable to all Americans, the prison population wouldn't be overcrowded. But there is a darker and more sinister side to this. And that is, prison has become a dumping ground for the mentally ill. In the 90s the government decided closing down mental health institutions in favor of erecting more prisons was a bright idea. Simultaneously, the word "Prisoner" was replaced with "Inmate." And prisons became known as institutions.

They blame gang culture, and that could very well be the

case, but sending people to prison who should be in mental hospitals equally adds to the dangers of prison life.

H-5) *The hostage situation!* Hostages are held against their will. Hostages are uncomfortable. Hostages endure great duress and immense suffering. Hostages are always planning a way to win even when they aren't winning.

I've been held hostage for all of my twenties, all of my thirties, and well into my forties. And after 24 years of unjust incarceration, I hold the same disdain for prison today that I held the first day I was taken hostage.

Before it was too late, I became vigilant of my intentions and my purpose. For me, *it was education.* After acquiring a respectable level of comprehension, and being cheated out of my first opportunity to challenge my conviction, I gravitated towards the law library. Insignificant matters had no place in my mind. And the only thing that mattered was outliving this deprivation, and one day returning to my family and friends. And then, if my moves coincide with my intentions, I could make a positive impact in society.

My eyes have taken in a lot. At a tender age, and even more at an advanced stage. And I'm on board with my pain and my plight serving as a cautionary compass, supplying some sense of direction to the misguided.

Prison is what the person makes it. I've been at both sides of the spectrum: *hanging out and the hostage.* And I wish I had taken it serious from day one. My life would certainly be different today.

"I freed hundreds of slaves, could've freed thousands if only they knew they were slaves."

— Harriet Tubman, 1820-1913

Chapter Two

Mama's Baby

Mama's Baby

I had a friend (*female and a young mother*), with whom I was also romantically involved with, get into some serious trouble. While I was away on a trip, her apartment became the subject of a sting operation. She lived in a low-income housing complex in York, PA, called "The Jungle" mostly consisting of impoverished Blacks and Latinos. She had been arrested and charged with gun possession, and held on what was more like a ransom than a bail. That had been her first arrest and time hitting the York County prison.

Upon my return from New York, and almost as I was learning more about the details of the raid, her mother and father were pulling down on me. That hadn't been the first time I'd met the parents. They were a black family that was pretty tight knit, so her mother visited the Jungle on the regular.

"*My daughter is charged with weapons, and I have her son. Boogie, she needs a lawyer...*" *she had said with earnest and concerned eyes.*

I was nineteen at the time and I wasn't making the best decisions. Basically, I was learning as I went. But what was obvious and undeniable was that this beautiful Black queen had her daughter's back, her front, and a plan that consisted of making sure an adequate defense was put forth.

I hit her off with lawyer money that night, and her daughter, Nia Chance, never saw the inside of a state prison. Joanne Tyler Floyd was able to get her a county sentence of less than a year.

If friendship is not an opportunity, but a responsibility, then parenting is mandatory. Especially, during a crisis, such as becoming entangled in the criminal justice system.

The more we know, the more we grow. And this book is about constant elevation, while glaring adversity right in its menacing face.

Unlike my old flame, during my prosecution, I was without my parents. My father was serving a lengthy sentence in New York's DOC, and my mother had fallen back into her addiction while trying to raise six kids on her own. *Five of those six offspring were under the age of ten.* I believe she would have been there if she could have been there. Because my mother, Regina Crocker, has always believed in my innocence. She left this world (*liver cancer*), supporting me.

But the reality is this: *no kid should have to go through a prosecution alone. Certainly not a murder prosecution.*

One of the things I want to stress in this chapter is the importance of parents being involved when their child is being prosecuted for a crime.

Statistics show that the presence of a parent actually plays a critical part in the numbers and disparity in criminal charges and sentencing when comparing, based on race and class.

A recent report by The Sentencing Project, a Washington, D.C. research-based and advocacy center, found incarceration of Black Americans nearly five times the rate of white Americans, whereas imprisonment of Latino Americans is 1.3 times the rate of white Americans.

Criminal justice reform has gained much traction here in the U.S. in recent years. 21st Century civil rights activists and social justice warriors have attempted to place their palms on the pulse, while high profile celebrities have begun to extend their platforms assisting the wrongfully convicted in their quest for vindication.

Earlier this year, the National Registry of Exonerations reported 2,810 men and women to date have been wrongfully convicted of crimes in the United States.

What I would like to see added to this discussion (*criminal justice reform*) is the consequential effects when our youth are being prosecuted without parental involvement.

Here's the deal, most of those exonerated have served an average of two decades and were minorities. Most of the exonerated individuals weren't able to drink legally in America when they were wrongfully convicted. They were still *Mama's Baby* while being dragged through the court system alone.

These overzealous prosecutors recognize the absence of parents. They look back into the galleries of those courtrooms and see no concern and get diabolical. They turn to unfair applications of the law and venture into tyranny. Enhancing their reputation as a prominent prosecutor is the driving force, no longer justice.

Think of that man rolling slow, curbside, fiendishly readying himself to slip the side door of his van open to abduct an innocent child off the streets in broad daylight. He seizes the opportunity because there are no parents around to stop him.

Or, the guerrilla pimp who prays on the wounded mind of young girls, enslaving vulnerable children into the sex trade, never to be heard from again.

In both of these scenarios, the parents turned their heads for a moment too long. *And disaster struck.* The same thing goes on in the criminal justice system, only the crimes are for political gain.

My prosecutor went on to become a judge, finishing a 10-year term. He successfully ran for retention in 2013, securing another 10-year term, while I sat in prison wondering why God had cursed me. In 2015, he stepped down, (*or was forced to resign*), due to misconduct, depending on who's telling the tale. What he's been accused of was nowhere near as egregious the violation he'd done to my constitutional rights.

Now I want to lay out a hypothetical (*but true*) scenario that is not to offend or upstage anyone. I'm just speaking the truth. Fiona (*white woman*) understands that District Attorneys (*even the ones who think they are little dictators because of the immense power they wield*) are the prosecuting officer of her judicial district, elected by the people. DA's come with an abundance of credibility. But, just like all other politicians, they too can be held to task to do the right thing—when it comes to our youth.

We live in a meritocracy here in the United States. Therefore, you earn the right to hold office by appealing to a majority of your district, city, country, state, and at the highest levels of government.

Fiona understands this. And may have very will helped vote the District Attorney into office. So, when her little Jonah finds himself in trouble, Fiona sets up a meeting with the District Attorney to express how one bad decision shouldn't determine the rest of Little Jonah's existence.

Fiona attempts to soften the hardened criminal image local media is capitulating by attempting to separate Little Jonah's societal potential from the criminal act setting him back.

Fiona may be very disappointed in Little Jonah for being arrested and held without bond. However, Little Jonah's court proceedings are now on her day planner, and a top priority for the family. And the outcome is just as important to her as it is to Little Jonah. By the time Little Jonah's case is scheduled for trial, Fiona has worked vigorously to see that Little Jonah is not given a raw deal. In fact, the prosecution is so tiresome with her advocacy, they offer a befitting and appropriate plea deal. Fiona convinces Little Jonah to plead out. And, for killing someone in cold blood, Little Jonah receives 10 years. He'll be home by the time he's 29 years old.

Meanwhile, Little Rakim's mother, *Purple*, isn't as savvy when it comes to politics as her rural area contemporary, *Fiona.* Purple isn't sure what the District Attorney's actual function is. She doesn't know that she can request a meeting with the District Attorney in the interest of her child. Most occupants of "Urban Renewal" America are not educated in politics, elections, and the purported purpose of lower-level government officials. We assume that the purpose of the District Attorney is to flip our people and prosecute our families and friends when that is not always the case.

Little Rakim walks that alone, very few visits from family and his attorney, rushed through the process, and ends up with a life sentence.

The two scenarios I depict here are the realities of poor and disenfranchised people versus white privilege.

A white kid and Black kid could be charged with the exact same crimes and inevitably receive contrasting penalties. Little Rakim will more times than not receive LIFE WITHOUT PAROLE, for his homicide, while Little Jonah is given a plea that says he is redeemable. This is not the sole correlation of race and class, but principles of parenting too. Knowing this, I have to speak out. I know white boys who had better outcomes because their parents were visible and vocal when their child got in trouble with the law. If a prosecutor senses that a Defendant's parents doesn't care how things turn out, that kid's constitutional rights become mince meat for that rising star within the DA's office. Little Rakim and young men who look like him become throwaways in the quest for political power.

I hear it all the time—"*You do the crime, you do the time!*" Well, a woman I respect and admire immensely told me, "*You don't have to be a boy scout to have Constitutional rights...*" What that means is: *you're still entitled to Due Process and a fair trial.*

Young Boys, young mothers, we have Constitutional rights! It's not just white men punishing us, Roger King (*ex-Philadelphia prosecutor*) put more black men on death row than any prosecutor in the country.

But we contribute to the ridiculously high levels of racial and ethnic injustice when we abandon our youth in times of need. We suffer inequality *and* disproportionately.

In August of 2021, President Judge Clark, a Black woman, of Allegheny County here in Pennsylvania spoke out about the racial disparity and systemic racism in the criminal justice system and the need for cure. (8/25/21 TribeLIVE.com).

While white supremacy and capitalism punctures the vital organs of humanity, it equally complicates the workings of the American justice system. I say that because it feels as if the American criminal justice system never ceases to assure that minorities get the short end of the stick when clearly so much is needed.

This is not subjective banter; this travesty is supported by numbers and facts.

Blacks get the worse attorneys, the worse healthcare, the worse jobs, and the worse schooling.

The war on drugs specifically targeted and affected no culture or caste of Americans more than it has Blacks. From the racial profiling to the over-policing, to the malicious prosecutions.

America's minorities, encapsulated by "*Urban Renewal*"—*a move that segregated the city of New York by wealth and race*— were and are people of limited options. Public housing, public school and public assistance did two resounding things to the people of my community during the 80s: *it created complacency, and it birthed instinctual hustlers.*

Urban Renewal was an experiment (*project*) that began the boom of *housing projects*, *Section 8* and today's more modern versions of *low-income housing*. It was spearheaded by one of America's most influential figures in post-war New York, beginning in 1931. The term "*Urban Renewal*" derived from an English author by the name of George Orwell, pseudonym

Eric Arthur Blair. He lived from 1903-1950.

One thing is certain about the experiment: poor brown people would be found there. And anywhere there are poor brown people, drugs and violence are not far away, unfortunately. Just think of what Jay-Z said in his book "*Decoded,*"

"No one hired a skywriter and announced crack's arrival... But when it landed in your hood, it was a total takeover... Sudden and complete..."

Now, imagine growing up in an environment where no one's getting ahead except the street dudes, and your young eyes witness firsthand the rewards of ruthlessness. Then take into consideration that for 250 years Blacks were unable to attain wealth here in America, while our white counterparts had a 250-year head start. And even in present time, non-ideal existence is a reality for minorities. *So, we take to the streets, and we join the underworld, just to become targets of law enforcement.*

Knowing this, we have to be vigil of the righteous vultures interested only in protecting heritage, lest we lose more of Mama's Babies to a broken system absent of justice and equality.

"To have been a criminal is not a disgrace,but to remain a criminal, that is a disgrace."

— Malcolm X

Chapter Three
Grinding All My Life

Grinding All My Life

Ghetto movie star, a hood celebrity, playboy, gangster, a kid kingpin, and eventually murderer. By the time I was 20-years old, I'd been called all those things.

But "murderer" wasn't given to me by the streets; that came from the Commonwealth of Pennsylvania. *And I have always refused to accept it...*

The 90s was a very ruthless time in the streets. Gangsters, guns, drugs, and violence was front and center. What I didn't see in my neighborhood was an abundance of FATHERS. Growing up with just a struggling mother was to a lot of us a curse, because once we were a certain age (*thirteen*) they gave up on trying to mold us, even though we were still very malleable. Instead, mothers gave that attention and guidance to the younger siblings.

Leading up to my arrest, prosecution and wrongful conviction, my life was very tumultuous. Lots of ups, and almost as many downs. But once I figured things out, I became known for two things: *getting money, and being with beautiful women.*

I started having a lot of money around the age of seventeen. And I was putting a lot of dudes on. The OGs said I was ahead of my time. The legendary dudes was taking me to lavish nightclubs, on boat rides, to shows, and giving me tips on how to stunt. I had a Rolex, I was driving hot cars. Can't omit the immaculate wardrobe that would rival today's drip. And this was all the rewards of being part of a criminal underworld.

Where I come from, crime was a way of life.
That's why movie producers depict it in film; that is why rappers lace their lyrics with the underworld happenings.

I grew up mired in poverty, where opportunity was limited, and the streets were pretty much all we had.

I'm quite sure we all know the famous Jay-Z lyrics from "*Can I Live*":

Can't lie, at the time it never bothered me,
At the bar, gettin' my thug on properly
My squad and me, lack of respect for authority
Laughin', hard, happy to be escaping poverty, however brief...

I made a lot of bad decisions in my younger years. The most critical was dropping out of school in the eighth grade when I was thirteen. The crazy shit is, I was on the verge of finishing that grade. I'm no quitter by any stretch of the imagination; I just didn't know it bac k then.

Today, our youth have so much opportunity. If you can read, and you can write, and you can communicate, you can make a better life without crime being the only source of light.

Education changed the trajectory of my life. And I often imagine *what if I had given myself a chance at schooling in the streets???* The answer is: *I could've run a successful company with my street smarts combined.*

Street smarts can take you far in the streets, but traditional education, comprehension and understanding must accompany the street smarts in prison.

While we're running those streets, we have no clue that there exist characters within the criminal justice system who can make it seem and feel like an inhumane institution with a penchant for punishment, instead of justice. An inhumane institution that never viewed the Constitution as a document applying to poor brown people. An inhumane institution that allows people who shouldn't be inside prison to wither away behind prison walls.

The first time I saw a dude get shot I was twelve. It was in the corner store bodega, and the gun was pressed against his head when the sound jarred me. "*Pop!*" I was standing in line when the dude's body slipped from a stance to a slump. The dude didn't die, but he was never the same. *And, neither was I.*

I started hustling when I was ten, going on eleven. Late 80s. That first hustle, I'm not so proud of. But what I will say is: *it was creative and not my idea.* My mom's (*may she rest peacefully*). It was summertime, the sun hadn't risen yet, and she took me on a stroll. When that walk was over, we had two shopping carts filled with cans and bottles. We returned them to the corner store for the five-cent refund. We hit them with about 400 spent cans and bottles; they gave her $20. Wasn't much, but it beats broke. Then I started bagging groceries at the local supermarket. On a quick glance, I recognized that bagging groceries wasn't as embarrassing as picking up spent beverage containers. (*My peers gave me hell for both*). If I pulled up at the supermarket everyday after school, I could pull $100 a week easily. That happened only a few times, me putting a full week in, shoppers blessing me with quarters, nickels, dimes, and dollars. Things were rough at home. And in ghetto America, when things get rough, *the government starts making decisions for the family...*

I hustled in Queens. But by then, I was in foster care, and slipping into the streets. No more collecting cans, no more packing bags. I sold my first piece of crack when I was twelve. I was called a pitcher because I went hand-to-hand and made a buck off of every $10 vile of crack I slung.

I hustled in the Bronx. But taking things was much easier, so I did Jux until I got sent away for 12 months at age 14 for taking things that didn't belong to me.

I got money in Maryland. Now that was higher learning. The cat who invited me out there was on his way to becoming a millionaire in 1993. All off street money. He was twenty-two when I joined his team. I idolized this dude; in the same way that Bleek had Hov. But I wasn't interested in being his protege long term; I wanted to be just like him. Smooth, brass, smart, interesting, ambitious. I took everything I learned, and I started moving on my own. Every car I saw him drive; I would eventually have in my small fleet.

I bubbled in Charleston, SC. It was far, and I would get homesick, but dope money is swift flows, much different than what I was accustomed to. So, I made the trips work.

Now, I made most of my money in Pennsylvania, the streets of York, where I also took the biggest loss of my life. By eighteen, I was moving $30,000 a week in coke. I hustled from dusk till dawn. It was there that I saw my first $100,000. *Money that was mine, all me.* It wasn't easy. Nothing ever was for me. I always had it hard. Today, as I sit in prison, an acclaimed writer, things are still hard for me. On my momma, York was good to me. It changed my life in a good way, and in a bad way. *The gift and the curse.*

But I wasn't just a drug dealer, I was a businessman. Just in the wrong business. Nevertheless, business is business in America. *Until you get caught.*

If I could talk to 19-year-old Ty Boogie today, I would say, "*Watch them niggahs that's close to you...*"

Right after my 19th birthday, my mother's apartment had been burglarized. In that break-in, I lost $34,000, ten grand in jewels, approximately ten grand in leather jackets and North Face coats. My entire Jordan and Air Max collection was also hauled away.

Surely, it was God's Plan I do not know who had masterminded the heist. Surely, God knew my heart was pumping the kind of passion that never produces anything good.

Prior to that incident, I'd done everything in my power to get money, and avoid prison. But that philosophy had been somewhat compromised, the jubilation I had been experiencing from my street success had been replaced with paranoia.

Unfortunately, my mother's house wasn't just burglarized, but I was framed by my best friend shortly after that. I was also deprived the luxury of having genuine people in my corner when I was at my lowest. And it ultimately impacted the performance of my attorney, and the potential to get a fair trial.

I want to say something to all the dudes in the streets living the fast life and no exit plan. When the authorities come, and you have no bail, the prize possessions you sacrificed your freedom to acquire no longer belong to you.

The main reason my trial attorney motioned the court to withdraw as counsel two months before trial wasn't just because I rejected plea offers, but because my peoples had retained him and never dropped another dime off. The whole time I was being prosecuted, I was told he was being paid when he really wasn't.

You know what that got me??? *Constructive denial of counsel and left me vulnerable to prosecutorial misconduct.*

We never spoke on the phone while I was awaiting trial. And he rarely visited the prison.

That anger and disdain I was submersed in nearly corroded my belief in God and constructed an unwilling atheist.

I believed that injustice to the government was loved and embraced and even celebrated in the very way they imagine crime is to us. Because I know the evidence against me was demonstratively false, and nefarious conduct was center stage.

No one can prepare you for the rigors of prison life. Because there is no one way of doing time. And things constantly change.

Prison will change you.

Prison will change your appearance.

Prison will change your perspective.

Prison will change your entire being.

You could very well leave prison just a semblance of yourself if you are not mentally strong.

Or you could leave prison in a pine box, hence ...Death by Incarceration...

If I was going to overturn my conviction, I would need to

learn the law. Which meant, I would also need to elevate my comprehension skills, and my ability to absorb knowledge. So, seven months after my conviction, August 13, 1999, *first try*, I obtained my GED.

Just as oatmeal is better than no meal, a General Equivalency Diploma is better than no diploma. It was a small achievement compared to the ultimate goal, but it was a start.

The next thing I wanted to do was— find peace. *Not with the way the criminal justice system was failing me, but with the challenges of becoming an adult in prison. And, being estranged from my family.* There was no telling how long it would take to win a new trial, or how long it would take before me, and mom spoke again after she had squandered the remains of my quick cash. And finding that peace would have to come from talks with God. So, I went to church and read the Bible, then I visited the Mosque and studied the Qur'an. I prayed, I fasted, I gave charity from what little I had left in this world. And I still hadn't arrived at a place of peace. No matter how much piety filled my soul, it wouldn't heal the pain. (*And to this day, I believe in the oneness of God. But I also believe had I been a prisoner of religion, I would not be the man I am today. Religion can be more restricting than criminal law. I needed fluency, especially when I was already up against restraints.*)

I wanted out, vindication, and I would not be scrupulous

in my efforts. Not only was I ambitious about my freedom, but I was also determined to make something out of myself while in this situation.

Successful people don't wake up and roll out of bed and into a windfall. They work. They sacrifice. They remove limits from themselves. *But most importantly, they reinvent themselves.* And they not only understand this concept, but they personify it—success by association. When you run with the big boys, people automatically assume you're in the (club...). The big boys, I'm talking about are mental giants...

The new grind begins!

"What you spend years building, someone could destroy overnight; build anyway..."

— Mother Teresa, 1910-1997

Chapter Four

The Main Stumbling Block To Relief

The Main Stumbling Block To Relief

In the Commonwealth of Pennsylvania, LIFE means "*you will die in prison*" because you have been condemned. The only exit from one of their 20-plus prisons after being sanctioned as such is through the courts by winning a new trial.

Today, there are approximately 5,500 lifers in the Pennsylvania state prisons. Most have never killed anyone and are banished as accomplices.

On January 15, 1999, after being convicted of First-Degree Murder, by an all-white jury, I received a LIFE sentence as an accomplice.

I'll never forget that day, as it resides in infamy. I was wearing a gray sweatsuit and gray Foamposite Nike sneakers, because my trial clothes had been rejected by the York County Prison's mail room. And I recall thinking, *my life as I knew it is over!*

In a SCI-Somerset day room, the fall of 2011, I opened and read a letter from an attorney. My hands seemed to tremble like a lone leaf dancing against a rugged wind, and all the noise around me turned to utter silence. One of the four post-conviction lawyers who had represented me over the years described my plight as:

"*The biggest problem with your case has always been*

the evidence that you attempted to shoot (Dude) the alleged object of the conspiracy, in the head but failed to do so only because the gun jammed.*

"This is the most damning possible evidence in a case like yours involving a non-shooter with no connection to the victim.

"Although you were not charged with attempted murder, I believe this was a calculated decision by the prosecution to keep you on the hook for the meaningless killing that did occur, which lacked a shooter."

The 100-plus prisoners in that Somerset day room, autumn 2011, hadn't ceased all the hooting and hollering; *everything except my ability to see had just seemed to pause.* And, I had to agree...that testimony supplied by my closest comrade was the most damning possible in my case. It had also become the albatross around my neck, infecting all judicial rulings against me, and inspiring several denials of relief.

There is no disputing that I did not fire the shots that ended the life of the man I have spent decades in prison for killing. In fact, at the time the man was shot, I was not in the vicinity.

However, the prosecutor's theory of culpability as it pertained to me was that I was an accomplice because I put a gun to another dude's head and face (not the decedent) and pulled the trigger, but the gun jammed.

** Dude is a part of court records, if you so wish to know his identity.*

On Monday, January 11, 1999, trial was set to start, and moments before the trial was to begin, the prosecution for the (*first time ever*) advised Defense that my best friend of ten years and codefendant, Danny Steele, AKA "Dirty Danny," AKA "Joker," would be testifying that moments before a man was shot, I put a gun to another dude's head, pulled the trigger and the gun jammed.

Danny wasn't just some imaginative fabulist, who exaggerated and embellished, he attributed to me the quintessential murderous act. *Whether the gunman succeeds or not, with evidence like that, the intent to kill is established.*

After receiving this evidence on the day of trial, I sought to have trial counsel request a continuance and trial counsel expressed that a continuance would not be allowed. Counsel then leaned over and whispered, "*You have to take the stand and testify on your behalf, to refute the new allegation. And everything else he has lodged against you; or you will never be free again.*"

My refutation not only included me denying trying to blow someone's head off, but also a meeting in a motel room just an hour before.

Danny had gone biblical, told the jury, "*Some say the Lord saved him, because the gun jammed right in his face.*" I witnessed the ashen look on the faces of those twelve white jurors, and I knew I had no choice. He had the entire jury fascinated by his tales.

By this time, I trusted trial counsel as much as I trusted Danny Steele. Two months before trial was to begin, trial counsel had filed a Motion to Withdrawal from my case. The trial court ultimately denied it because we were so close to the trial date, but counsel's actions said he had withdrawn anyway.

One of the few times he had come to the prison to visit me, it was on behalf of the prosecution. Court ordered, *100 times I signed a handwriting sampler so the prosecution could establish that I indeed was at the Super 8 Motel prior to the shooting.*

Nevertheless, I thought he was advising me correctly when counsel urged that I testify. And, I mounted the stand to proclaim my innocence. I didn't know what he would ask me, but I admitted to being at a dice game where the initial shots had been fired. I told the jury that I was there only to squash the tensions, not to kill anyone. I denied being a gang leader and downplayed my illicit street activities. I emphatically denied meeting at a hotel to plan the killing of a rival gang leader. I looked the jury in their eyes and told them, I did not try to shoot dude in the head.

No physical evidence was introduced to establish that I used a gun, nor was any evidence presented to prove that I fired any shots that night. That's why the meeting at the motel was so critical to the prosecution's case, and that "gun to the head and face" testimony.

At 19 years old, October 1997, Danny Steele was the first person charged in this crime.

I was arrested in 1998.

Danny Steele received 2-1/2 to 5 years for his testimony. The judge thought that Danny had earned his sweet plea deal by supplying critical testimony that led to the conviction of the people most responsible for the decedent losing his life.

The 2-1/2-year plea deal had come up in hopes of impeaching Danny, based on the fact that Danny had wrote a letter to the DA's Office expressing what he expected in exchange for his testimony. However, prosecution denied it when the prosecutor told the jury, "*The only deal we have is we pitched one of the charges, but the same amount of time for both charges.*"

The implication was that Danny was facing 20 years, when he was never in jeopardy of facing 20 years, or life.

And for his dishonesty, he was rewarded with 2-1/2 years in prison. A plea deal the prosecutor withheld from the defense, and the jury.

In 2014, Danny died in a car riddled by bullets. Shortly before that, he recanted his false testimony, revealing that he was under immense pressure from prosecutors when he testified.

An open plea that hinged on how well he testified hovered

above his head. Danny was street smart, but he was also illiterate. So, I believe him when he said when his story didn't make sense or wouldn't amount to a First-Degree Murder conviction, he just kept adding things: *things the prosecutors knew were not true.* So essentially, they encouraged the false testimony.

A fictitious motel meeting.

The fabricated eyewitness accounts.

Danny's dying declaration was that he perjured himself repeatedly, which led to my wrongful conviction of First-Degree Murder.

Appreciation took up temporary residence in my spirit for him coming forward with this information, but it did not correct the wrong I suffered because of his dirty games.

Three years after Danny's demise, my godson was charged with Danny's homicide, tried, and eventually acquitted. The motive was that Danny had refused to recant.

To corroborate Danny's recantations, I hired private investigators to locate and interview two potential witnesses.

A-1 Investigations would locate the Super 8 Motel clerk, who rented me the motel room. She corroborates Danny that no meeting took place there, and that the room was actually rented well after the time of the shooting.

Private Investigator Donald J. Tracy was successful at locating and interviewing the dude Danny said I tried to shoot in the head and face.

We learned that the dude had testified about this incident already, back in 1998, at Danny's Preliminary Hearing, in which his testimony was absent of "*a gun being put to his head and the trigger being pulled.*" The prosecuting attorney had the opportunity to hear that testimony prior to the commencement of my trial.

All indications lead to the fact that I was wrongly convicted. Had the jury known Danny was testifying falsely, had they heard the testimony of the two unavailable witnesses my investigators tracked down, had they been made aware that he would only serve 2-1/2 years, I would not have been convicted of Murder 1. I would not have spent 24 years in prison.

Danny Steele's lies could have been proven to be false 15 years before his death had my trial attorney conducted the simplest investigation. But there was no pre-trial investigative work done on my case. *None!* The very first time any investigations were done on my behalf, I had five years in.

My entire adult life had been taken, and every attempt I made to reverse this manifest wrong, the York County District Attorney's Office met me with fierce resistance, clinging to the lies as if their lives depended on it.

What society at large may not know is, *when a prosecutor decides to give credibility to a cooperating witness, that prosecutor is tasked with the obligation, in the interest of justice, to investigate any and all evidence supplied by the cooperating witness before presenting it in a court. The entire plea deal relies on the truthfulness of the information.*

"Tysheem put the gun to his head and his face, and went to pull the trigger, but the gun jammed. [sic] Some said the Lord saved him. Because the gun jammed right in his face..."

This testimony was pivotal in establishing that I had specific intent to kill, a requirement necessary to hold a non-shooter responsible for a homicide he didn't commit himself. Shared intent does not meet that threshold. The prosecution must prove beyond a reasonable doubt "specific intent to kill," for accomplices.

At a hearing in 2013, the trial judge recognized that testimony, categorized that testimony, emphatically acknowledged the "gun to the head" testimony as—THE MAIN STUMBLING BLOCK TO THE DEFENDANT'S RELIEF.

The judge knew that fabrication was the very fact keeping me imprisoned. He had presided over the trial. He knew it...

There was a plea deal for me on the table the day trial began. All degrees of homicide would be dropped if I pled guilty to Aggravated Assault, in exchange of a sentence of 10 to 20 years. After Danny testified, and right before I took the stand, trial counsel approached the bench and told the judge that he thought I should take the 10 years. The judge said, "*I won't do ten years now, I've heard too much. The best I will do now is fifteen.*"

Danny's testimony had that kind of impact! Not only on the jury, but also on the judge. It was jarring, theatrical, but most of all *damning!*

When I tell my story, and people hear that my codefendant (*turned Commonwealth's star witness received 2-1/2 years for his cooperation*), brows raised, jaws drop, and I am reminded that life isn't fair. I am reminded that I would rather have one true enemy than 100 fake friends.

The promise of 2-1/2 years to save himself was just too good to pass up on. The promise of 2-1/2 years to a codefendant in a murder case was unheard of. It's indicative to how weak their case was, and how important the grandest results were.

It is my belief that my case was more about political aspirations than it was about justice. The 90s was the era of lock-emup and throw-away-the-key. My case was fresh off the war on drugs, and the tough on crime climate in America. And, what they thought they understood about me personified SUPER PREDATOR.

I believe my prosecuting attorney aborted his mission of justice, and ventured out on another, not so noble, and concerned with neither truth nor Due Process.

Its fulfillment meant life in prison for an unwise street dude, whom the facts say was no saint but also says was no murderer.

A street dude whose acts admittedly made him subject to a proportionate penalty but not the banishment I received.

A street dude en route to that judgment constitutionally entitled to, but deprived of, prosecution by authority unwilling to stand upon the shoulders of known falsities when evident truths would not elevate him to the heights it might wish.

I would be remiss if I didn't mention that Danny is the lone eyewitness to the homicide. The prosecution presented no other eyewitnesses to this back alley shooting death of the murder victim. No one corroborated Danny's testimony to how the homicide went down. *Everything rested on Danny.*

We started out as friends, *me and Danny*, hustling together in the streets. And when it mattered most, we were opponents, me against him. And the prosecutor told the jury to not believe me, to not trust my refutations, but to find Danny credible, *and to believe the motel manager (who really knew nothing).*

*****

When I think of judges, I think— "*How did I get myself into this jam; where my life, my liberty, and potentially my sanity comes down to what he thinks of me???*"

Judges are supposed to be arbitrary, impartial, taking no

sides, just there to oversee a controversy between a state and a defendant. But for me, it never felt that way.

During my prosecution, and 20 years of post-conviction litigations, I never felt like I was just going up against the prosecutor. I always felt like my trial judge was never going to do the right thing.

There were times I knew I was in over my head, as a Pro Se litigant, but I was still competitive because accepting this fate was not an option...

Back to these judges...

In August of 1998, a hearing was held to test the evidence against me. Defense counsel and I were still on okay terms, and he filed for a Habeas Corpus Hearing, asking that the charges be dismissed. At the end of that hearing, the trial court ruled that *the Motel meeting, if believed, did not establish conspiracy to commit murder, but conspiracy to commit Aggravated Assault.*

Defying that ruling, the motel evidence still became the centerpiece of the prosecution's case. The judge had not overruled his August 1998 factual determinations. And, with no objections from defense counsel, I was denied Due Process.

In criminal law, judicial rulings are binding. *And no one is above the law.* Was that judicial bias or prosecutorial misconduct? *Both.*

To further add insult to injury, the motel manager was

not cross-examined, nor was he asked by prosecution to specify what time the room was actually rented. The answer would have corroborated my defense, and discredited Danny's accounts. That's why the prosecutor didn't present the question.

The prosecutor closed his case with:

"*You heard the testimony of a motel manager who says that on the 5th, not at 12:30 on the 6th, on the 5th, Shondell, Shamble, Tysheem Crocker, checked into the Motel 8 in York...*"

The fake motel meeting went from discussing assault to conspiracy to commit murder 1.

During jury instructions, the judge specifically told the jurors that *if I did not go to the motel room before the shooting, I would not be part of the conspiracy to commit First Degree Murder.*

"Counsel points out that I talked about agreements at the motel, and then they went down and did some actions and what you could infer from that. Counsel pointed out that I didn't mention that well, at least one of the Defendant's said he was not at the motel till 12:30, and if he wasn't at the motel, then obviously he couldn't have any agreement. Well, when considering all the possibilities, frankly, I left out the obvious. I don't think you need me to tell you that if he wasn't there, then obviously, he wasn't part of the agreement."

This jury instruction holds no effect when the prominent prosecutor is telling the jury, "Don't believe the Defendant, believe the motel manager."

Then there was witness testimony from prisoners coming forward whom Danny had spent time within York County Prison. According to them, Danny was telling a story contrastly different than the one he told the jury on January 12, 1999. At least one of those witnesses said Danny told him he committed the homicide because the decedent owed him money.

Again, I wasn't present for the murder, so that could have very well been true.

In response to those guys coming forward, the prosecution told the jury, "*Tysheem, the leader of the Cream Team, is a very big guy down at the jail, and these guys want to be on his good side, that's why they are here testifying today.*"

The Cream Team was my crew. A crew I'd never proclaimed myself to be the leader of. I may've been the most ambitious, I may've had connects, but I wasn't leading anyone. All my homies were bosses in their own right. But that there was the motive: *Gang Leader tries to kill Rival Gang Leader, innocent bystander killed in the process...*

At the time of my trial, I didn't see it. I was 20 years old, and totally oblivious to the law. (*They say ignorance to the law is no excuse.*) Today, I am awoken, and I see clearly...

That theory was red meat for an all-white jury: Black boys from New York caught in a plot to kill a rival gang leader and anyone with him.

My case was treated as if the victim was an innocent bystander killed in the midst of a "drug war." My case was treated as if we were fighting over drug turf. But that truly was not the case. Me and the hustle had a love/hate relationship. I loved what the hustle was able to provide for me and my family; but I hated what it could do to a community. Yet, no evidence of my illicit street activity supported such a theory that this was a "drug war." However, temptation got the best of the prosecution. And he misled the jury, he misrepresented the facts, and he misplaced his duties to the Constitution in doing so.

When the actual facts of my case are reconciled with the inescapable conclusion that the alleged conspiratorial meeting at the Super 8 Motel **NEVER TOOK PLACE,** leaving only the alternative "spur of the moment" conspiracy theory suggested to the jury by the trial judge, the notion of imputing someone else's (*unwitnessed*) behavior onto me becomes even more egregious.

And I know someone losing their life is also inescapable, but you can't send people to prison for life who are not responsible.

Trials are not supposed to be prefect, but they must be fair. That is a Constitutional guarantee for any and all

Defendants in the American tribunal. Defense attorneys have an obligation under the United States Constitution to provide a full and zealous defense on behalf his or her client. The prosecution is responsible for all members of his or her team, and most importantly the testimony of ALL prosecution witnesses.

Prosecutors remain responsible for duty under BRADY to disclose favorable evidence to Defendants regardless of whether police investigators failed to inform prosecutors of evidence, as prosecutors can establish procedures and regulations to ensure communication of all relevant information on each case to every lawyer who deals with it.

I didn't know these things when I was being prosecuted. *And a lot of young defendants don't know these things*. That's why I think it is important to walk in another man's shoes. It is also important to understand another man's plight.

This is a perspective piece containing strong opinions and profound facts. This is a piece about perseverance and survival. I am a foster kid, and I am a runaway. I'm a junior high school dropout. I was a stickup kid and then a crack dealer, all before I was wrongfully convicted of murder.

Through me revealing my upbringing and circumstances, you know I'm just a fleshed out, three-dimensional human being, and a deeply flawed one. But nowhere near as flawed as the American criminal justice system.

"It is far better for a man to go wrong in freedom than to go right in chains."

— Thomas H. Huxley, 1825-1895, Eng. biol.

Chapter Five
Criminal (Law) Minded

Criminal (Law) Minded

Sometimes it's gonna be "the best you can do" that matters, and not the "outcome." Use the adversity to refine the path to the ultimate goal, which is redemption and liberty. And recognize—no one owes you anything.

The law library at SCI-Mahanoy was flanked with freedom fighters and jailhouse lawyers the first time I walked in there at 23-years of age. These men weren't hiding their litigating ability, or their briefs writing prowess, they were promoting themselves. These dudes were blunt and outspoken about the injustices being doled out to Blacks like it was candy. They spoke with conviction and was receptive to different points of view. Almost in the same way you would see in a banter filled barber shop in the hood. Picture LeBron James on *THE SHOP*, sitting around, sipping wine with his celebrity guests. Only, these unlicensed litigators were wearing brown prison uniforms instead of designer threads, discussing legal findings and conclusions, the difference between a holding and dicta, changes in statutes that bar prisoners access to the courts, and which Justices penned the best opinions.

The law library was like a galaxy of knowledge. But at the same time, it felt like the resting place of thousands of lost cases.

After a few visits, I found out most of the men had already served decades, had exhausted their appeal rights, and searching for new cases to come down that would give the courts jurisdiction of their cases again. Their bitterness and frustrations were being channeled into something positive. And to me, that was not only courageous but contagious.

There were a couple of *Bozos* in the mix too; fucking up unknowing dudes paperwork. *Beware of those dudes*. If he's (*or she's*) asking for chips and cookies—think about it—attorneys don't take chips and cookies. *In prison a person can pass themselves off as anyone*.

I got fooled once, and the dude wanted 10 bags of Wise chips—*plain*. And 10 packs of Famous Amos chocolate chip cookies.

The opening line of the Motion *Bozo* wrote for me said, "*In the Year of Lord*." I filed that and because my appeal was still pending in the State Supreme Court, the trial court dismissed it as premature. *That was a blessing*. Stuff like that is not an anomaly—*dudes filing motions and petitions on behalf of the uninformed individuals*.

When I really began to learn and understand criminal law, I was about 26 years old. *Law is not about truth, but more so about the prevailing party telling the best story*.

Through my studies, I learned that the criminal justice

system had never been perfect. The American criminal justice system is as flawed as all the other institutions governing this nation. *If they can't get healthcare or immigration right, then why would the justice system be flawless?*

God doesn't make mistakes. I didn't lose so much just because. But, for a cause. And I truly believe that part of my calling is *Awareness*, and enlightening this "*Awoke Culture*" who could truly benefit from inside information when it comes to the perils of prison and the American criminal justice system.

John Adams, when crafting the Declaration of Independence, thought that Democracy should mean "*fairness with a justice system that is the envy of all.*" And, in the evolution of this democratic republic, "*public education is supposed to be the cornerstone of Democracy.*"

That is just another reason why me writing this book is so important. I am speaking from experience, in a tone that can be accepted, with a tongue that can be recognized, in a fashion that is not stylish but fearless. *I am speaking truth.* I am *highlighting deficiency. I am conjuring up solutions.* And like Rod Wave, in this book, *I am wearing my heart on my sleeve.*

I stand in solidarity with all who have been unjustly jailed, falsely accused, wrongfully convicted, and the recipients of inadequate counsel.

I stand shoulder to shoulder with all the men and women who sacrificed their lives and liberty for a piece of the American Dream.

*****

I couldn't find any cases mirroring mine on the books. Nothing even remotely close. So my journey switched to studying the *Rules of Evidence.* That led me to cases that were overturned for insufficiency of the evidence. Cases where new evidence had emerged after the conviction that contradicted the evidence against the Defendant at trial. And cases where new evidence reduced the degree of guilt. That got me to really thinking!!!

At trial the exhibits entered into evidence contained the initials T.A.F. *No one questioned that.* For the sake of closure, I needed to know what the initials stood for, and who they belonged to. I remembered an attractive white woman being at the front desk of the Super 8 Motel where I'd been accused of holding the conspiratorial meeting, but nothing more. I wanted to know if she was contacted by the Commonwealth, and also would she have testified on my behalf had attorney Smith called her as a witness. *That could mean a Brady violation, and an ineffective claim.*

So, I put a $1,000 together and hired Walter Lee of A-1 Investigators to get some answers.

In May of 2003, Motels of America turned over employee

timesheets, and the full names of all desk clerks who worked at the Super 8 Motel the month of October 1997.

The initials on the EMPL OYEE TIME SHEETS were identical to the MOTEL RECEIPT used at my trial. It was clear Deb Sierra would have been at the desk at the time they said I rented the room, as she worked 3:00 PM-11:00 PM on October 5, 1997. And Teri Ann Flinchbaugh had come on at 11:00 PM, working until 7:00 AM.

This was New Evidence. This evidence contradicted the evidence presented to the jury. No motel meeting, where a shooting was alleged to had taken place, no premeditation... which is necessary to establish First Degree Murder.

Most people don't even know the definition of PREMEDITATED MURDER. *And sadly, I was once one of them.* I was 24 when I learned that it means: *planning the means and opportunity to kill before the fatal confrontation has begun. The sinister aspect of this element is not just the planning of it beforehand, when there is not yet a confrontation to alert the unknowing victim that his/her life is in danger. It's planning to kill someone before they can know of the necessity to defend their lives.*

Deliberation means: *considering the legal jeopardy—detection of the crime, the potential interrogation and arrest, possible imprisonment, eventual prosecution and conviction, and even as far as the possibility of death by incarceration—*

and making plans to avoid that jeopardy. That's as complete as a killer's state-of-mind can be.

Together, the two elements show the deadliest state-of-mind a killer possesses—*planning to kill unknowing victims and then getting away with it.*

But we must also take into account, it is beyond the cognitive capacity for a non-shooter, with no connection to the victim, to think that way. Thus, the only way a non-shooter with no connection to the victim can be convicted is if a prosecutor creates something to fill the g aping hole. That something is an overt act, or they can't prove every element of the crime beyond a reasonable doubt.

*****

People have been asking me to venture into nonfiction for quite some time now. And I wasn't sure I had a unique enough voice, or a perspective rich enough for people to be willing to invest their intrigue into. Wasn't sure I had even experienced enough; if I had achieved enough. It is one thing to pen a novel, and a whole other thing to become a voice colliquating ideas, concerns and criticisms. But, like all the hurdles in my complicated life, I'm moving on instinct.

No disrespect to the court appointed attorneys who do care and take their profession seriously. But there are a large number of lawyers who be doing the least. And here's what I've experienced...

They play on a defendant's illiteracy to the law, they're malcontent because they're not getting the big bucks, they're flaky, uncommunicative, uninterested, and dismissive. They file more No-Merit Letters (*refusing to litigate on the defendant's behalf*) than they amend Pro Se petitions.

These functions or dysfunctions can really be damaging for wrongfully convicted individuals dependent upon a court appointed attorney to protect a defendant's constitutional rights.

My first court appointed attorney was assigned to my case November of 2000 to represent me on my First PCRA.

I filed a Pro Se petition, boiler plate claims with no knowledge of the law. Because I was illiterate to the law, he was supposed to amend my PCRA. Not as a favor but because I was entitled to effective assistance (*a rule-based right.*) But he didn't amend, nor did he review my case-*admittedly*. This attorney based my initial PCRA on a partial recantation by the star witness in my case. *At the time, I thought this was great.* But guess what??? Recantation is the most unreliable form of New Evidence here in the Commonwealth of Pennsylvania.

That petition was dismissed in open court. My first timely PCRA petition, that first opportunity at collaterally attacking my conviction without having to meet one of the three stringent exceptions to the TIME BAR was squandered.

Then that attorney abandoned me; never appealed to the Superior Court. The standard of review for a dismissed PCRA petition is limited to "whether the record supports the PCRA court's determination and whether the PCRA court's decision is free of legal error." *Com. v. Lawson*, 2014 Pa. Super. 68, 90 A.3d 1, 4 (Pa. Super 2014).

I had to report my attorney to the Disciplinary Board because he was ignoring my letters of inquiry. To my surprise, he admitted that he had abandoned me, allowing for the 30-day time limit to file the Notice of Appeal to lapse.

That was my wake-up call, the moment I realized this was going to be a rough ride. And that I would have to step my game up. All the information I discovered over the years could have been uncovered during my first PCRA had I been represented by competent counsel.

Fellas, females, you can file as many PCRAs as you want. But only the timely ones (*filed within that one-year window preceding your direct appeal*) will be heard lest you meet one of the three exceptions to the TIME BAR. See 9545(B).

I filed a 2nd PCRA citing "New Facts" (*abandonment*) asking the trial court to find that attorney ineffective. And the trial court ruled in my favor. Inevitably, the trial court assigned a new attorney to my case. She was a Black woman with very little experience in criminal law. Especially homicide cases. Her expertise was social security claims. But she did the best she could. By then, I had linked with a fierce legal mind and my education in criminal law began.

On appeal, I was allowed to file the claims he failed to litigate, which were ineffectiveness claims. *We were unsuccessful on appeal.*

However, that woman assisted me in uncovering one of the most critical points in my case. By providing me with a Subpoena Duces Tecum, she helped me initiate the investigation into the false claim that I had rented a motel room where I held a conspiratorial meeting about murder. It was she who had helped me uncover the identity of that Super 8 Motel clerk. She also retrieved Danny Steele's sentencing transcripts for me.

She wasn't a bad attorney, just in over her head. *Once the courts found out she was helping me outside of her court ordered duties, the court removed her from my case.*

My belief in the American criminal justice system was now as strong as an infant's grasp, because it should not be like this. When someone is sentenced to life, that person should not be depending on the dregs of the legal profession to represent them properly. And when that person could possibly be innocent, that person should not be representing him or herself.

*****

The best attorneys were once public defenders, civil rights attorneys, and legal aids. They are passionate about the craft. They leave law school looking to make a difference in the world.

It takes those competent attorneys 7 years to earn a law degree. That leads me to these questions:

(1) *What in the world was legislature thinking when they put in place a "one year" window for filing a timely PCRA???*

(2) *Did they really expect a convict from meager beginnings and a miniscule educational background to rise to the level of an attorney in one year?*

The answer to both of those questions is: *FINALITY*. That's all they were thinking about.

That is the very reason the win percentage on PCRA is extremely low in Pennsylvania. Not because petitioners aren't entitled to relief.

By the time I was able to comprehend the law, apply, and write legal arguments, I was already in prison for nearly seven years. By then, my initial PCRA had been squandered and I was filing my 3rd PCRA based on a Brady violation. *The prosecution had failed to disclose benefits offered to secure Danny Steele's testimony.*

That is the reality for thousands and thousands of Blacks and Latinos here in the Omnipotent USA. And we get stuck (*no way out*) because of inadequate representation. Yes, we get the *dregs* of the profession. *Attorneys anyone with money would never hire.*

The best time to beat a case is not post-conviction, but before the conviction. But if you have to file a PCRA, here are some of the things you need to know, so that you may be successful. These are things I wanted people to tell me when I was 20 years old, and clueless about criminal law. And especially post-conviction.

A PCRA must be filed within one year of the date your conviction becomes final. You can file as many as you want in that one-year timeframe. The trouble with getting in court begins after that one year expires.

This deadline is subject to statutory exceptions, including government interference, newly discovered facts, and a newly recognized constitutional right.

The most common cited exceptions include the suppression of evidence material to the defense, failure to disclose benefits offered to secure testimony, new evidence, and recantation. Recantation is the most unreliable form of new evidence and happens to be severely scrutinized.

Any form of new evidence must be presented in a PCRA petition within one year of locating the information. The affidavit must be attached to the petition. The evidence must be admissible and produceable.

People need to know, and this is legislative intent, counsel's ineffectiveness does not escape the PCRA one-year time limitation merely because they are presented in terms of current counsel's discovery of the "fact" that a previous attorney was ineffective. 42 Pa. C.S. §9541-46.

It is well settled that allegations of ineffective assistance of counsel will not overcome the jurisdictional requirements of the PCRA. *Com. v. Gamboa-Taylor*, 562 Pa. 70, 753 A.2d 780, 785 (Pa. 2000).

New facts alleged in a petition involving claims of counsel's ineffectiveness are not recognized as "new facts" under the PCRA statute. *Unless of course abandonment is involved.*

Interweaving a claim of ineffectiveness with the newly discovered facts exception as a means of establishing jurisdiction is unavailing.

For instance, the fact that *Bennett* was successful on appeal in the Third Circuit Court of Appeals does not constitute an exception to the time-bar.

Now, legal decisions can only overcome the PCRA's timeliness requirements in the context of Section 9545(b)(l)(ii) [a newly recognized constitutional right]. *Com. v. Kretchmar*, 2018 Pa. Super. 143, 189 A.3d 459, 467 (Pa. Super 2018).

Again, this is directly connected to Supreme Court rulings, (*state and United States*), that would have to be deemed *retroactive*.

The *Bennett* case, after he'd served 30 years,was decided

by the Third Circuit, not the PA Supreme Court, or the U.S. Supreme Court. Therefore, the case does not meet the statutory requirement regardless of whether it was held retroactive.

Bennett specifically discusses and addresses the jury instruction given when a defendant is on trial for first degree murder, as an accomplice. See *Bennett v. Superintendent Graterford SCI*, 886 F.3d 268 (3rd Cir. 2018).

The trial court's jury instructions violated the inmate's due process rights under U.S. Const. Amend. XIV, because the instructions were at least ambiguous and inconsistent and there was a reasonable likelihood that the instructions relieved the Commonwealth of its burden of proving the specific intent to kill required for a first-degree murder charge.

While a state may choose and decide to define Murder One, the United States Constitution required proof beyond a reasonable doubt of every element necessary to constitute the crime. *Due process is violated when a jury instruction relieves the prosecutor of its burden of proving every element beyond a reasonable doubt.*

Pennsylvania law requires that each defendant have the specific intent to kill for a first-degree murder conviction, as an accomplice.

An accomplice or conspirator cannot be convicted of first-degree murder based on the specific intent to kill of the principal. 18 Pa. Cons. Stat. §2502(a).

You have the right to effective assistance of trial counsel under *Strickland v. Washington*, a landmark case which included the first Black U.S. Supreme Court Justice... Thurgood Marshall.

<u>Strickland Ineffectiveness Standard</u>

To succeed on a Sixth Amendment claim of ineffective assistance of counsel, defendant must show that there is a "reasonable probability" which is a probability sufficient to undermine confidence in the outcome, that but for counsel's unprofessional errors, result of the proceeding would have been different. U.S.C.A. Const. Amend. 6.

Not that defendant would have been acquitted, but a different verdict.

A court need not determine whether counsel's performance was deficient before examining prejudice suffered by defendant as a result of alleged deficiencies. U.S.C.A. Amend. 6.

If there is only one plausible line of defense, the court concluded, counsel must conduct a "reasonable substantial investigation" into that line of defense, since there can be no strategic choice that renders such an investigation unnecessary. Id. at 1252.

The Constitution guarantees a fair trial through the Due Process Clauses, but it defines the basic elements of a fair trial largely through the several provisions of the Sixth Amendment, including the Counsel Clause:

"In all criminal prosecutions, the accused shall enjoy the right to a speedy trial, by an impartial jury of the state and district wherein the crime shall have been committed, which district shall have been previously ascertained by law, and to be informed of the nature and accusation; to be confronted with the witnesses against him; to have compulsory process for obtaining witnesses in his favor, and to have the assistance of counsel for his defense."

The person who happens to be a lawyer is present at trial alongside the accused, however, is not enough to satisfy the constitutional command.

These standards require no specific application in order to define counsel's duty to investigate, the duty at issue. As the Court of Appeals concluded, strategic choices made after thorough investigation of law and facts relevant to plausible options are virtually unchallengeable; in any ineffectiveness case, a particular decision not to investigate must be directly accessed for reasonableness in all circumstances, applying a heavy measure of deference to counsel's judgment.

Counsel's actions are usually based, quite properly, on informed strategic choices made by defendant.

An error by counsel, even if professionally unreasonable, does not warrant setting aside the judgment of a criminal proceeding if the error had no effect on the judgment.

The result of a proceeding can be rendered unreliable,

and hence, the proceeding itself unfair, even if the errors of counsel cannot be shown by a preponderance of the evidence to have determined the outcome.

Accordingly, the appropriate test for prejudice finds its roots in the test for materiality of exculpatory information not disclosed to the defense by prosecution, *United States v. Agurs*, 427 U.S. at 104, 112-113, 96 S.Ct. at 2397, 2401-2402, and in the test for materiality of testimony made unavailable to the defense by Government deportation of a witness.

The ultimate focus of inquiry must be on the fundamental fairness of the proceeding whose result is being challenged. In every case the court should be concerned with whether, despite the strong presumption of reliability, the result of the particular proceeding is unreliable because of a breakdown in the adversarial process that our system counts on to produce just results. 2069

"...the prejudice standard announced today does not erect an insurmountable obstacle to meritorious claims, but rather simply requires courts carefully to examine trial records in light of both the nature and seriousness of counsel's errors and their effect in the particular circumstances of the case."

*****

I hope this information is helpful to all who decide to pick up this book.

Over the years, I've heard a lot of entertainers say that

"they have no regrets." And, I've heard just as many public figures say "they live with regrets." I've been on both sides of the "regret pendulum." And as I got older, gained a bit of wisdom, I faced the reality that I do have regrets. One regret is not taking that plea deal of 10-years offered to me in 1999 just hours before my trial was to commence.

Had I accepted the plea, I would have been free at the age of 29. Instead, I've been imprisoned for 24 years.

I have publicity stated on The Lady T Show, March of 2021, "*There is nothing more important to an innocent person than their innocence.*" Regretting not taking the plea, in no way means my innocence is not the most important thing to me. Nevertheless, *decisions should be made based on intelligence and not on emotions.* And when your closest comrade is framing you, the intelligent move to make is to avoid a trial. Live to fight another day. Because when the government wants you, right and wrong is out the window, justice is subjective, and life is not always fair.

The Assistant District Attorney who prosecuted me, Thomas H. Kelley, knew I had not taken a life, that's why my plea would have been reduced to Aggravated Assault, *all degrees of homicide dismissed.* But, if they can make the facts fit, your life as you know it could very well be foreclosed.

Because I mentioned *Brady v. Maryland* in this chapter, and this chapter is entitled CRIMINAL (LAW) MINDED,

I can't close without touching on the analysis. *It was information that kept me going all these years.*

BRADY ANALYSIS

The concept of "due diligence" plays no role in Brady analysis. To the contrary, the focus of the United States Supreme Court had been, and it must always be, on whether the government has unfairly "suppressed" the evidence in question in derogation of its duty of disclosure.

All favorable material ought to be disclosed by the prosecution. To hold otherwise would, in essence, add a fourth prong to the Brady inquiry, contrary to the United States Supreme Court's directive that the courts are not to do so.

3 PRONGS

(1) The evidence must be favorable to the accused, either because it is exculpatory, or because it is impeaching.

(2) It must have been suppressed by the state, either willfully or inadvertently.

(3) The evidence must have been material such that prejudice resulted from its suppression.

The touchstone of materiality is a reasonable probability of a different result. Materiality does not require demonstration by a preponderance that the disclosure of the suppressed evidence would have resulted ultimately in the defendant's acquittal. Rather, a reasonable probability of a different result is shown when the government's evidentiary suppression undermines confidence in the outcome of the trial. The prosecution's obligations under Brady extend through all phases of the case. That's a fact! Even throughout Post-conviction proceedings. See Com. v. Williams, 732 A.2d 1167, 1175-1176 (Pa. 1999). "The burden of proof is on the Defendant to establish that the Commonwealth withheld evidence. A prosecutor is not required to deliver his entire file to defense counsel, nor is a prosecutor's duty to disclose such that it would provide a defendant with a right to discovery." Com. v. Burkett, 5 A.3d 1260, 1268 (Pa. Super 2010).

In my eyes, the suppression of evidence is just another form of oppression. And oppression is a direct attack on one's mind and sense of self. Protect your interest, and protect your neck.

On his deathbed, when asked, “What is your last message to the Negro?”he said, “Agitate, agitate, agitate.”

— Frederick Douglass, 1817-1895

Chapter Six
The Birth Of A Brand

The Birth Of A Brand

There's an Old African Proverb I would like to initiate this chapter with. It's a testament to the resilience of Black and brown people. It's a reminder of our willpower. And a reality no one can deny: Our people had been mired in a myriad of malicious injustices for centuries, yet we never stop being creative and courageous and innovative... "We the people, led by what we know, are willing to do what's thought of as impossible, for the ungrateful, and for so long we have done so much with so little, that we qualify to do absolutely anything with all of nothing."

I began writing books to save my life. At the time, my young mind was all over the place: *The women I'd dated, the clubs I'd partied in, the money I'd blown, the betrayals, the get-back, how the man who represented me at trial had forfeited my constitutional rights because I didn't want to plead guilty.*

Prior to my arrest, I was lit! My team was like the Lox without the lyrics, The Roc without the conflicts. Our studio was the block, our records was the rock. *We got the pictures to prove it.* Flix are not just about flexing, they're proof of existence.

There were other inspirations that solidified the commitment to becoming a storyteller, like reading literature I identified with, written by people I could absolutely relate to, but my decision to become a writer was born out of desperation. On some 50 Cent *ish, WRITE OR DIE!* That's how I truly felt. Like, *the only way I'm going to come up out of this darkness is by establishing a voice that exceeded prison walls.* If I didn't, then no one would know me outside these walls, and outside my teenage years. I would be just a memory and silenced forever.

I began writing then I began to think branding. S.G. Publishing is more than a brand. It's a passion, purpose, and necessary...

Year 2002, I'd been in prison for four years when I had come across a book written by a Bronx native who had also traveled some of the same cities and towns I had. That book was *B-More Careful.* I then read *Dutch*, written by Kwame Teague. *Coldest Winter Ever* had fell in my lap as well. And these cult classics led me to believe *I could do this too! I will do it!*

I was really in the streets. I was a rising star in the game. I had my palm on the pulse of the culture. I went through a murder trial. I've battled injustice! And now, I had a great relationship with education. I wasn't just street smart anymore; I was book smart too.

At first, I was met with some discouragement. From a couple of my comrades. As I would spend summer evenings in the yard—*studies done, workout completed earlier that day*—myself and the bros, I would share my ideas, my thoughts, my concerns. They would be met with quips, such as, "*What you gonna name this book, The Hottest Summer Ever??? Be Even More Careful???*"

And that laughter that followed those quips would just inspire me even more. As Timothy Ferriss wrote in his book *The 4-Hour Work Week*, "Most people are fast to stop you before you get started but hesitant to get in the way if you're moving," it played out just like that.

I beat my comrades into submission by being willing to do what they thought was impossible. However, I was after much more than the approval of my goons. I was writing for my very existence. I was moving like a freight train.

The writing was a release from my dark reality, an opportunity to prove I am more than a drug dealer, and it ignited another form of courageousness.

As I stated in my introduction, imagination is its own form of courage. Courage allows for vision, forward thinking, and immense possibility. My imagination was working 80-hour weeks. No lunch breaks. No roadblocks. No distractions. I focused on course until satisfied. And once I was too satisfied, I set out on another mission, another story to bring to life.

I wanted my freedom back, vindication, and there would be no limits on those effects. Quite frankly, I had become addicted to the fight. *Write or die!*

Now, when you're funny, you can be sarcastic. And that dude was wildly funny. "*The Hottest Summer Ever???*" Even I laughed later that hot summer night while in my prison cell. But I got the last laugh.

Not one, not two, not three, (*in my LeBron James voice from the Miami Heat press conference*), not four, not five—I have published nine books, including six solo projects under my own imprint. That catalog includes some classics such as *Respect The Struggle* and *Street Generals*.

One of the most critical lessons I learned over the years is: *things take way longer to materialize than we would like them to. And, when they don't pop immediately, that doesn't mean you're not doing everything possible to achieve satisfaction.*

My vision began with one book (*Respect The Struggle*) an ode to my generation (*the 90's*). It's about the struggles of growing up fast in the fastest city, self-identity, personal growth, and finding purpose in a place where gaining respect is a must.

I finished the manuscript the beginning of 2004. And while in solitary confinement the summer of '04, I started work on the script for Street Generals Part 1.

I had already been accustomed to sending out thirty to forty letters monthly. I just added some of the high-powered writers of Hip Hop/Street Fiction to my mailing list.

By 2006, I was in direct contact with Shannon "Supa

Shan" Holmes (*B-More Careful*), and Wahida Clark (*Thugs And The Women Love Them*). Both of these National bestselling authors were considered rising stars in the urban fiction world at the time. Today, they are legends. I credit both of the writers as being early mentors of mine, because I learned so much from them. Wahida had actually given me my first (*and only*) rejection letter. With it came a personal letter containing some life changing advice. The next time I sent her a script, she said, "*The title alone got me open, Ty.*" That was the beginning of my rise as a viable voice in street fiction. But before that, Triple Crown (Hip Hop—Fiction's Motown Records) was in play.

At the time, I had no idea Shannon Holmes was one of their top executives, responsible for helping brand K'wan and Nikki Turner. By the time we linked up, Mr. Holmes was moving to Simon & Schuster and kicking big boy dialogue.

Back to Triple Crown...

I remember the conversation like it was yesterday and not seventeen years ago...

"*I got some good news for you.*"

"*Okay,*" *I said slow and calmly. Rob Weisman was my main man, my only true support system, and he was not only helping me with basic necessities, but also with paying my lawyer and shopping my first book.*

"*Ty-Boog, Triple Crown called, and they want to publish*

your book, man."

"*What???*"

He responded with laughter, nothing heavy, just a light chuckle that was more cunning than anything.

"*Was it Vickie Stringer???*" *I had asked huddled over the phone on the wall of cell block I-Unit at SCI-Mahanoy, in Frackville, Pa.*

"*Her assistant. She had a baby; I could hear crying. Like a newborn or something.*"

Every other day, at the same time, I would call Rob at his flagship clothing store in Harrisburg, PA. Back then, phone cards weren't in effect yet, and collect calls were $8 statewide, and $14 to New York. I didn't use the phone much.

"*Dead ass?" I had shot back in shock and holding the phone close to my ear as if I would miss something.*

"*Yeah, man," Rob said smoothly.*

Rob is one of those smooth Jewish dudes who came up on the streets (hustling) in the 90's. One of my fondest memories of us on the streets is, me linking with him for the first time when we were both teenagers. We had a mutual friend (Razor Reynolds) who brought us together the summer of 1996 on some money moves.

I'm in my green and gold (two-tone) 4-Wheel Drive Mazda MPV, and he hopped out a white one. Both vans were clean and sitting on big chrome shoes. I remember thinking,

This white boy is eating.

The solid gold Cuban link and medallion on his neck was almost as thick and icy as my $10,000 neckwear.

This is the mid-90's, and to have an MPV at that time meant you were probably moving weight. And he was definitely doing his thing.

Chambersburg, PA seemed slow to me, but we became fast friends, building a bond that lasted the test of time, most of which I've spent in prison. (*He visited me on Rikers Island, SCI-Camphill, SCI-Mahanoy, and the Tombs.*)

Robert had photocopied and packaged my first manuscript at Kinko's and pushed the copies out to potential publishers of street fiction. One day on one of the visits where he was trying to wreck my physique with all the cheeseburgers and pizzas and sodas, he would have filling the table, I asked him to help me start my own publishing company. At the time he was building his family and branching out to other cities with his HAT ZONE franchise. He had gone from a hustler to having a legitimate empire (*7 stores*) in select cities of PA. Even opened one in Baltimore.

He never told me "No," but did stress he knew nothing about the publishing game. I tried mailing him any and everything I could get my hands on about publishing. But he just wasn't interested.

There was never a follow up call from Triple Crown, and

I believe my ambitions were becoming too much for Rob.

When I visualize, I am undeniable. An effective plan was fermenting in my mind, and I had a business plan too. So, I decided to bet on myself. I had already moved the crowd in the hardest place to prosper (*prison*) with the hardest audience to satisfy (*prisoners*).

In a weird twist of fate, I would meet a man who would not be intimidated by the grandiose ideas of a dude who hadn't been on the streets in nearly a decade and had no release date in sight. Instead, he would gravitate towards my ambitions. He had a Harlem, New York savvy I hadn't seen in a long time. One that was cultivated in instinct. He had his fingertips on the pulse of the culture: *music, fashion, film*. Everything my wandering mind was focused on. He, *Omar Jennett*, was my sister's boyfriend and child's father.

Naquan Crocker and myself are the firstborn of my mother's eight children, just two years separating us. In 2006, she had decided to make that three-hour trip to Pennsylvania to see her big brother for the first time locked in a cage. And, you guessed it, she was denied entry because they claimed she wasn't on my approved visiting list. She had traveled all that way on a van and could not see me.

When we spoke that night, she said, "*I'm never coming back out there again.*" *She's stubborn and ambitious just like me*. Glad she chose to be a nurse and not the street life.

The "*never visiting*" remark wasn't true. She would end up visiting me 100 times. But that's where Omar came in. He had joined the conversation saying, "*I got a Expedition. Put me on the list, I'll bring everybody.*"

While they were planning the next visit, I sent a printout of my approved visiting list to my sister with her name on it so that she could never again be denied entry.

After a series of visits and conversations, tossing ideas back and forth, in the SCI-Mahanoy visiting room, S.G. Publishing was formed. And together we began work on the structure and functions of the company. I didn't have much money, but I still had 200 grams of 14K gold in the form of a Cuban link and bracelet, an iced-out crucifix, as well as a Rolex. *S.G. Publishing startup!!!* After ten years of holding on, anticipating my release, I finally decided to get rid of the last of my worldly possessions.

Now, we were ready to roll and introduce me to the world as novelist BOOG DENIRO. My freedom was connected in every way too.

But I wound up spending most of 2008 in solitary confinement for some prison politics. (*I hadn't begun to feel like a hostage yet*). Having just met Omar a year earlier, I felt like I let my family down. While they were trying to help me, I was jailing and hurting myself with bad decision making.

When I was released from *the jail inside the jail*, I was

at a new penitentiary and re-establishing myself. The first person to visit me there was Omar, along with my sister (*his-soon-to-be-wife*).

The challenge was: to not lose focus of my dream. The fame to me was as important as a foxhole is to a dead man. I cared about reclaiming my voice. A lot of people don't realize this, but a big part of a prison sentence is silencing the prisoner. So, having a platform was necessary and essential if I was ever going to prove my innocence.

With the company's name incorporated, Omar assumed the role of Chief Operating Officer. He saw it as us building a brand. The highly coveted CEO title belonged to me. And I saw it as us assembling a megaphone...

In 2010, *RESPECT THE STRUGGLE* went to print, and was released to rave reviews. In addition to being on Barnes & Noble Bestsellers.com list, Amazon.com, Omar had brokered a book-selling partnership with BLACK STAR MUSIC & VIDEO, (*a Harlem, New York staple at the time*), and my books were flying off their shelves.

My books were also selling out in URBAN LEGENDS, the first black owned bookstore in York, Pennsylvania. Jemell "Casper" Hill, my cousin, was the owner of that establishment.

The first two rounds of print sold very quick. Every female I knew from my past life purchased *Respect The Struggle*. I would wonder, *Do they think I wrote about them???* (*There were many, many females.*)

In a DMX move (RIP) at the behest of Lyor Cohen (*Def Jam 1998*), Omar said, "*Let's drop your second book now!*"

And we put out two books in one calendar year. My second release is titled "*STREET GENERALS, No Sellouts*." That book sold out fast too.

The buzz was so crazy, I got offered the cover of *WHY Magazine*. This was the premiere issue, released at a party hosted by *VH-1* vixen Jessica Rabbit. She'd been on the *Real Chance of Love*...a competitive dating show.

WHY Magazine was a street periodical intended to enter a market *FEDS Magazine* and *DON DIVA* had dominated for years. The owners of *WHY* were street dudes, so I felt like they would do it right. The owners of this particular periodical were looking to bring legendary stories of the 90's street scene (*movers and shakers in Central Pennsylvania's streets*) to a hungry audience craving the facts. My story was already a big deal because of how it had been sensationalized in the news in 1998 and 1999.

A month after we did the interview, the premiere issue of *WHY Magazine* was published. They gave me 100 copies off the rip, and my team put them to use. Book sales experienced an up tick. People I hadn't heard from in over a decade were reaching out, and the federal courts just so happened to be reviewing my conviction at the same time.

It felt like I had regained my voice, my sense of self, and I'd be remiss if I didn't say this—*I was changing the narrative.*

And then came social media!

Game changer!

If you want to make moves in today's society, you're going to need a powerful tool at your disposal. And that just so happens to be social media. *Millennials* and *Gen-Z's* have made social media their personal playgrounds. Facebook, Instagram, Twitter, TikTok, YouTube, Snapchat, etc. There's a story I love and particularly pull inspiration from. *Snapchat had been deemed a bad idea by corporate giants. But Evan Spiegel (creator) had unrelenting belief. Look at Mr. Spiegel today.*

From prison, I have managed to not only embrace this boundless form of technology, but also make use of the many platforms advantageously. Of course, it's a proven and viable method of keeping in contact with friends, family, and acquaintances, but to me it was much more. It was a lifeline. Thank God for the internet!

Having a visual presence in today's society is particularly important when you're trying to bring attention and awareness to injustices and inequalities. In my case, it was being wrongly convicted by an all-white jury. So, I needed these platforms to get the help necessary to uncover new information and evidence.

It is world knowledge that the wrongfully convicted stand at a great disadvantage when it comes to finding evidence and gathering new information where excellent investigation is a necessity in order to uncover exculpatory evidence.

What worked for me is my honesty, by being forthcoming, and then a level of consistency. As you know through my own confessions early in this book—early on in my struggle I would not volunteer the details of my case and conviction. You gain followers, supporters, and even shares by being authentic. But never appear obsessed and overly consumed with attention. That signals insecurities, and insecurities drive followers away. *Social Media shared in my rebirth.* I no longer held fears of being rejected and/or abandoned because of my sentence. I was empowered through the ability to release all that I had repressed for a decade.

Back in 2006, Wahida Clark introduced me to the concept of *PLATFORM.* You cannot be successful as an incarcerated writer without a platform, she had preached. *No platform, no book sales.*

For me it was deeper, I was building a brand. *And that brand was FREE BOOG.* I needed help, I needed aid, assistance, and real advocacy. And to my surprise, there was an interest for what I had to say, what I wanted to share, *and a real interest.* Writing novels and powerful pieces about social injustice, inequality, wrongful convictions and Black empowerment got me the attention of community activists, influencers, and celebrities. But most importantly, the *Pennsylvania Innocence Project.*

In 2015, when I mentioned to my right hand man Omar, "*What do you think about a CHANGE.org Petition about my case?*" I was taking a huge leap of faith.

Omar Jennett replied, "*It can only help!*"

Omar is the optimistic type. Omar doesn't need to be convinced of anything because he is an instinctual being full of life experiences. So, I wasn't surprised he was on board with my idea. What surprised me most is his commitment to my cause. Of course, he was invested because we were business partners, and he was now married to my sister, Naquan (*they wed in June 2010*), but he believed in my innocence wholeheartedly. *Never wavering.* We didn't have a lot of money to give a law firm, to fork over to a Certified Legal Investigator. We were Black owned, moving units independently, but still a small operation. However, we were rich in spirit. Rich in ideas. Rich in determination. And sometimes that's worth more than the bag (money).

So, my suggestion could be looked at as the *Hail Mary's of Hope* (to use a football terminology). Without hope what seeds are we planting??? What foundation are we erecting upon??? The Universe doesn't conspire against us, but the Universe also will not go out and line up a bunch of green lights. We have to mix the hope with action.

As fate would have it, after pending from February 2005 till December 2008, my 2254 Federal Habeas challenge to my conviction had been dismissed, and the District Judge did not issue a Certificate of Appealability. Devastated, I still filed a notice of appeal with the Third Circuit Court of Appeals. And after 18 months (January 2009-July 2010) the Third Circuit certified 2 of my claims of constitutional violation.

(1) Whether trial counsel failed to investigate the false accusation that I met at a motel prior to a murder to conspire?

(2) Whether the trial court violated my constitutional rights by instructing the jury that I could be liable for a murder that I was not present for by transferring intent???

In November of 2011, the Third Circuit did not grant the requested relief.

All claims (constitutional violations) you would like to have reviewed in Federal Court in a 2245 Federal Haheas Corpus Petition under the AEDPA (Antiterrorism and Effective Death Penalty Act) must be preserved in state court or the claims will be procedurally defaulted. President Bill Clinton signed the AEDPA into law on April 24, 1996. This piece of legislation was suppose to expedite death sentences, eliminating frivolous filings. But it actually is a contributing factor to mass incarceration as it prevents wrongfully convicted people from seeking relief just as it would a guilty man. Timothy McVeigh and his domestic terrorism was the catalyst for the bill, though he had actually welcomed the death penalty. My people, you only get one bite at the apple.

Between the U.S. Middle District Court of PA, and the Third Circuit, I'd been litigating for seven years in federal Court.

The pursuit of happiness and the need to experience the best of the world had again been stunted.

The longer a prisoner is down, the harder it becomes to get your case reviewed and overturned. Most of the time, prisoners end up pursuing relief from their convictions as a Pro Se litigant. (Pro Se means, *individuals without legal representation.*)

To my surprise, the conversation with Omar would produce an impact of mammoth proportions. The CHANGE.org petition had circulated around the internet's many platforms through *shares* and *likes* and *retweets* and produced thousands of signatures. Attached was my upbringing, the changes I'd made since being incarcerated, my accomplishments, and the need for legal assistance. I listed the known misconduct that led to my wrongful conviction, and how the help of the public could bring change to my convictions.

People have been using this method of posting for some time now, and for various reasons. *To have laws changed, to have rules changed, to have conditions changed, to get the attention of the people with the power to make the changes.*

My Bro, Omar, tweeted the CHANGE.org Petition with all those signatures and comments at the Pennsylvania Innocence Project, whom in turn tweeted back:

We would like to hear from Mr. Crocker to see if we can further assist with his case. Please have him contact us by mail. 1515 Market Street, Phila., PA 19102.

That is the power of social media! And the power of thinking outside the box!

Around this time, summer of 2017, I had a PCRA Petition pending, my 4th, a hearing date scheduled, and two lawyers (Sandra Thompson and Roy Galloway) paid to represent me.

The judge reviewing a PCRA petition is oftentimes the same judge who oversaw the original trial. And from reading hundreds of cases, and my own experiences, the judges seem to think it is their obligation to issue reasons to deny the petition rather than reason to grant relief where viable claims of Constitutional violations or prosecutor misconduct really exist (undermining the confidence in the jury verdict.) Verdict means *speak the truth.*

Just so happened my trial judge had retired, and I had been reassigned.

Even though my trial judge had dismissed 3 of my previous petitions, I believe he would have granted relief on that one. My trial judge had been the jurist who classified THE-GUN-TO-THE-HEAD testimony as *the main stumbling block to my relief.* The prosecutor who represented the Commonwealth at my 3rd PCRA Hearing, said, "*If Tysheem's relief is going to come down to whether or not he tried to shoot someone in the head, then we need to hear from that person.*"

Now I had the dude saying I hadn't tried to shoot him in the head, and that was found to be *incredible*.

Classic case of—*when you get the answers, they change the questions....*

No one ever really gets used to rejection. But somehow one could expect it. For me, rejection ignited a revolutionary stance in me. *The Hurricane Carter swagger mixed with the 50 Cent aura.*

Anyhow, while all this is going on, my application is in with the Pennsylvania Innocence Project. I wasn't sure if anything was going to come of it, but it was in.

At the very same time the new judge was dismissing my 4th PCRA, August 2019, a letter was in route to me from Temple University, headquarters of the Project.

Legal Director Nilam Sanghvi was telling me to gather my legal documents so that when a legal intern or volunteer attorney was assigned, I'd be ready to ship. I was also advised that it would be a year or more before that would occur.

Less than a year from that correspondence, Leticia Chavez-Freed was on a secure line with me telling me things I'd been wanting to hear my entire adult life. "*...You are* *innocent. And we are trying to see what we can do, what options we have...*"

My dumb ass said, "*I was in the process of filing for commutation...*"

And she said, "*You accepting responsibility for a crime you did not commit is not an option.*"

I was just desperate, tired of suffering for a crime I didn't commit, mentally exhausted, and the then Lt. Gov. Fetterman had been all over the news encouraging prisoners to file. So, something I had never believed in had suddenly become my only option at ever knowing life as a free man again. COMMUTATION. *Or so, I thought.*

There would be no throwing myself at the mercy of the Board of Pardons. *I had landed my Legal Dream Team.* Civil Rights Attorney Leticia Chavez-Freed, Alexandria Lappas ESQ, Certified Legal Investigator Kitty Hailey, and Nancy Mahoney.

Even with all the things I was able to achieve, all the growth, when I got that call, I was at my lowest. I was out of options. And, then this happens.

As I am writing this book, I am still in imprisoned unjustly. But as of January 2022, my first counseled-PCRA based on excellent investigation was filed. New Evidence, Prosecutor Misconduct, Government Interference, and Actual Innocence highlight the request for relief.

At this current time, there is also a heavy *FREE BOOG campaign* going on online led by the legendary D.J. Cocoa Chanelle. Before delving into this criminal justice cause Cocoa has spent time at Hot '97, BET, MTV, VH-1, and she is a recipient of the *Black Girls Rock Award.*

But it isn't the records that she's spun on the hottest radio station, or the crowds she's rocked with Hip Hop superstars that has impressed me most about this incredible human being. Instead, it is the trip she made to Africa where she donated her time and resources for humanitarian efforts, feeding and clothing less fortunate children and families from impoverished villages. Talk about giving back... The world needs more people like DJ Cocoa Chanelle fighting for what is right, standing with those who have been dealt a bad hand, and using that star power to bring light to dark situations.

Highly controversial YouTuber Hassan Campbell is covering the story.

In March of 2021, Lady T of the Lady T Show based in Rocky Mount, NC, gave me my first opportunity to speak to the public on a live streamed show. *I had just landed my Legal Dream Team.*

Fresh Mix Magazine, owned by DJ Waffles of the Padded Room, also gave me an opportunity to speak candidly about my plight, my progress and my future plans in his online periodical.

Khalil Abdul Muhammad, community activist and founder

of Justice For Youth Foundation, New York based, gave me my opportunity to blog, where I wrote 20-plus pieces and articles on the topics of social justice, Black empowerment, wrongful convictions, and the need for criminal justice reform.

This is what hard work can produce. *Beanstalks have grown from seeds I planted nearly 20 years ago.*

It shouldn't be a mystery I decided to sit down and conduct some interviews myself.

Although, I have spent 24-plus years in prison, and I am more stoic than free flowing, I do have a youthful spirit, I am full of life, eager to learn and always ready to teach.

The first of the three interviews tackle Due Process. Then we discuss the purpose of the PCRA. And finally, commutation in Pennsylvania.

I'm trying to give back. God gives us gifts to share, not keep to ourselves.

As the educators of the eighties used to say on the streets of New York—Don't hide, divide...

"As long as you are putting out product on a consistent basis, demonstrating improvement each project,the fanbase is going to grow..."

— James Prince, Rap-A-Lot

Chapter Seven

Due Process ...

Due Process ...

The Constitution, a living and breathing document, seems to wink at our white contemporaries and the wealthy, while flouting at the less fortunate ancestors and kin of a historically deprived race. Well, actually it is not this sacred document itself showing favoritism, but its interpreters drawing a line between the beneficiaries of justice.

Where there's no law, there is no order.

You can find it in any of the Holy Scriptures.

It's present in the street culture.

But no one is more beholden to this code than the government. I say that because they really have no code. There's no real checks and balance for them. If they don't wanna give relief, they call a blatant error a harmless error. If there is glaring evidence that your attorney is a bum, they will say you suffered no prejudice by his failures.

I've lived these nightmares. I've breathed these nightmares. I relived these atrocities. And I decided that I wouldn't allow for this to break me when I survived one of the most vicious eras of the streets, *The Nineties*.

Year four of my conviction, I made a conscious decision that no matter how many times they try to shut me down, (the government), I am gonna keep coming. That's when I really took to criminal law and learning it.

One of the first laws of nature is self-preservation. As Mobb Deep marked in Hip Hop's history books (more than a quarter century ago), on the classic "Survival of the Fittest,"... *only the strong survive.*

I channel that track because to this day, I subscribe to that philosophy: *only the strong survive.* With that said, it is incumbent upon everyone convicted of crimes, and especially wrongly convicted of crimes, to add criminal law to their survival kit.

To know your constitutional and civil rights is far more valuable than knowing raps. And to protect your interests, which in legal terms means DUE DILIGENCE, is much more fulfilling than winning the flag football championship.

Now clearly everything ain't for everybody. With that in mind, I'm led to believe that when a person doesn't frequent the law library, when that person certainly should, it's not because that person doesn't want to, but because learning the law is extremely hard. And then of course, because most incarcerated people just don't believe the law can or will work for them. So, why waste their time??? When they can focus on that jump shot, or focus on that recitation or Holy Scriptures, or simply focus on nothing at all because that is easier than facing rejection. But when you understand that Due Process allows for you to be heard, you cannot silence yourself.

In this part of my first nonfiction book, I want to discuss

Due Process. I chose to wax philosophically about such an important topic with someone I respect on several levels.

One of the first things I noticed about this brother upon meeting him is—*he didn't have a lot of the neurotic things going on that me and my comrades had going on.* I'm talking—*PTSD, narcissism, anxieties, and/or phobias*—caused by rough upbringings and life on the streets at a young age.

Brandon and I became acquainted while trading Hot Shots. For those of you who don't know what a Hot Shot is, it isn't a bad batch of dope. A Hot Shot is a racy photo of a very attractive woman. Usually porn stars, strippers, reality stars, or a periodical model. At one point while incarcerated, I owned one of the priciest collections, as did this brother. I guess I might as well put it out there now: *I made a lot of money off of racy photos while incarcerated.* That was one of my many hustles before I became an acclaimed crime novelist. (*Brandon owns a Hot Shot business.*) Sex sells.

But yes, that is how I met my big bro Brandon Key. And we eventually began to collaborate on other things. But where we really clicked was when the fabulist who had framed me decided he wanted to recant the testimony that got me a life sentence.

The affidavit relieving me of any criminal culpability he had attributed to me had come at a time when I felt like the walls were closing in on me. I had already served 14-plus years wrongly convicted. Had filed two post-conviction motions, a 2254 Federal Habeas Petition, and my conviction had been upheld on every level of that appellate process. Hopelessness, desperation—*those feelings that led me to the streets in the first place*—were creeping back into my psyche, and with a vengeance...

Brandon was the counsel I sought out. I didn't want to squander or sabotage what could have been my last shot at freedom. And he walked that walk with me.

*****

Today, with his reading glasses on, bushy goatee, Brandon's looking like Malik El Hajj (had Malcolm X lived to see his fifties). When I express to Brandon what my eyes are telling me, he chuckles. It's always a good day when I can get him to release laughter. When you have served decades in prison there is rarely anything to find joy in.

Brandon is in his fifties. He speaks eloquently, but hints of assertiveness emerge when he is discussing law. And that is because he is enthusiastic about this complex and complicated bridge in our lives.

So, tell the readers where you hail from...B.K.

BRANDON KEY: The Wynnefield section of West Philadelphia.

BOOG: *That is the middle-class section of West Philly;*

where Will Smith also grew up. Correct?

BK: Correct.

BOOG: *What year did you catch your case?*

BK: 1996.

BOOG: *Will Smith hadn't become Hollywood royalty yet.*

BK: No.

BOOG: *I'm gonna start with this—do you feel like you got a fair shake in the American justice system?*

BK: Not at all. They tell us that we have all these rights, but that's just rap. They just run us through the system.

BOOG: *You're putting that politely. That's the gentleman in you. They fuck us over is what you really wanna say. Brown and black people, that is. They fuck us. How long did it take you to learn the law?*

BK: That's a hard question to answer.

BOOG: *Why?*

BK: Because the learning never ends. I'll just say that, if you have someone to point you in the right direction, you can learn the law pretty fast, but most of us don't have someone pointing us in the right direction, so it takes us years and years.

BOOG: *Years we don't really have because of the stringent laws in place to keep us out the courtroom.*

BK: Years we don't have.

BOOG: *You just said the learning never ends. From the day our conviction becomes final, we only get one year to file a post-conviction petition challenging the conviction. To me, that's almost impossible. Why? Because attorneys attend law school for a minimum of seven years before they can practice law. But legislative intent has destined that an uneducated kid, fresh off the streets, is required to learn the law in less than a year, file the PCR A petition, or face the consequences of being time barred. That is one of the leading factors why mass incarceration is castrating minorities: time restrictions on filing claims.*

BK: True.

BOOG: *You have a college education; how has that helped you in learning the law?*

BK: I don't think it's the college experience that helped.

BOOG: *Why not?*

BK: It's the early education that I was fortunate enough to have that 90% of us don't get. It's just having good English: being able to read, understand what you're reading, and having the ability to take what you are thinking and successfully transfer it onto paper. A lot of times a dude knows what he wants to say but because he doesn't have good English, when he goes to write it out, it's not saying what he thinks it does.

BOOG: *I'm an eighth-grade dropout. My education came from the streets. And out there in those streets the first thing I learned is survival. Hustle or die! My main hustle was narcotics entry level and on grander scales. That takes instinct more than anything. But, without that traditional education, strengths like comprehension is lacking. Which goes back to what you just said...for minorities with minuscule education it is much harder to learn the law. And the consequences are costly.*

BK: That is a huge problem for us who are fighting our own cases.

BOOG: *Afeni Shakur, mother of Hip Hop icon, Tupac, defended herself successfully after being tried with a group of Black Panther comrades in the early 1970s. They'd been accused of conspiring to bomb public buildings. That's the exception and history worth mentioning. You assisted me; is that something you do? Or, just for the chosen few?*

BK: Well, I'm retired now, but I did used to do law work; it was almost always for my homies. Because of the bond I had with these guys.

BOOG: *I spoke about our bond to open this interview.*

BK: We would always be talking about our cases anyway—the same way people on the streets talk to each other about whatever's going on in their lives. I would see that my homies were being fucked around, and I would try to help. From there, the natural next step would always be for me to become more and more involved in the case. So, there's a good handful of homies that I went through a couple appeal stages with. Most of them you know, and all of the cases became personal to me.

BOOG: *I do know. We've been on the same soil for over a decade.*

BK: My involvement in your case was/is different. We went to war with them for so long.

BOOG: *The government. The York County faction.*

BK: Close to ten years. And you were there shoulder-to-shoulder, mind-to-mind with me for all those years of reading, researching, strategizing, writing, typing, and so on.

BOOG: *I hate it here today as much as I did then, as much as I did the day I got arrested. That's why I go so hard.*

(There's a pause, time is taken to allow what I just said to marinate...)

BOOG: *I ended up in the restricted housing during that second PCRA we worked on. I had eighteen years in, and a critical witness in my case came forward.*

BK: Right.

BOOG: *I got five months in the box for a cell phone. And you made sure a beat wasn't missed in my absence.*

BK: Right. In the process, your case was a vehicle for us to really spend a lot of time buildin'—not just about law, but about life. So, I feel like any work that I put in on your case over the years was repaid many times over with the knowledge and inspiration that I've received from you. I feel like I was chosen.

BOOG: *I had a few OG's over the years. I been OG, but I only have one old head—and that is you, my guy. Speaking to you was/is what I imagine talking to a professor on a university campus would feel like.*

(There's that smile of modesty, Brandon always seems to reserve for the right time.)

BOOG: *Everything we did in the courts paved the way, got me to this point...December 2021. Next month, January 2022 the ChavezFreed Law Office will be filing a PCRA based on Actual Innocence, New Evidence, Prosecutor Misconduct, and a Brady violation.*

BK: I can't wait to see you walk out of here.

BOOG: *I be knowing. A victory for one is a victory for all.* (Brandon has this knowing smirk, one I've come to know well. Again, I've managed to awake emotional senses in this mental giant.)

BOOG: *We're here to discuss due process or, the lack thereof. You ready?*

BK: No doubt. That's supposed to be the basic foundation of American law, but it doesn't exist for us.

BOOG: *There is a large number of Americans, multitudes with family members incarcerated, so they wanna know what's going on inside these walls. How they can help their loved ones. And that likely stems from our record rates of incarceration. For every 100,000 Americans, 698 are locked away. The U.S. locks up more people per capita than any other nation. Approximately 2,300,000 people are incarcerated, according to Prison Policy Initiative. So, I'm gonna give them what they can't get on You Tube via Prison Lifestyle Videos, or a Podcast...Go-·head, Brandon...OVERDUE PROCESS.*

BK: When you are put in chains and sent off to prison, with the most serious numbers or life, you might decide that you have to put up your own fight to get back, whether you have a lawyer on the case.

BOOG: *I think we all had some bad lawyers.*

BK: Trying to learn criminal law is like touching down in a new city and trying to learn the hundreds of highways and avenues and boulevards and side streets and alleyways and shortcuts and dead ends. In the "city" that is criminal law, and all law, all these paths to freedom are said to be paved with "due process." But are they really?

BOOG: *That was heavy. There you go showing your genius.*

BK: Under the 5th and 14th Amendments to the United States Constitution, and similar parts of State Constitutions, every citizen is supposedly entitled to Due Process whenever the government is trying to deprive them of something in which the citizen has a right of life, liberty, or property. There are two categories of due process—procedural and substantive—but most of the time it is procedural due process that is everybody's focus.

BOOG: *Procedural due process is...?*

BK: Concerned with what steps the court should take in conducting a proceeding and coming to a decision. In other words, what type of process will make sure that enough care is taken in reaching this decision which will affect the rights of this citizen. The more serious the thing the citizen might be deprived of, the deeper the process that is due in order to finalize the deprivation.

BOOG: *And that depriving includes?*

BK: Anything ranging from the $25 or so it takes to pay a parking ticket, to 25 years of our freedom, to our right to LIVE and BREATHE (death penalty). In all cases though, two of the most important steps along the path of due process are—giving the person (1) notice, and (2) the opportunity to be heard.

BOOG: *Anything you want to add?*

BK: The second of those two rights.

BOOG: *Let's get it.*

BK: The opportunity to be heard. Almost no criminal defendant knows what that really means.

BOOG: *Okay, Bran about to get wild deep.*

BK: For almost twenty years, I didn't.

BOOG: *Told y'all this dude is deep...he got some notes.*

BK: When I did find out what it means, it was clear that

we don't have it. It's not real for us. There's a U.S. Supreme Court case from 1936 called Morgan versus United States, 298 U.S. 468. It's not a criminal case; it's about a federal statute—law—setting prices for livestock, cows, et cetera. Sounds crazy, I know, but I believe it is the most important case of the hundreds and hundreds I've read.

BOOG: *Why?*

BK: Because it breaks down what "hearing" is, what the "opportunity to be heard" is. Under the statute, when the Department of Agriculture made rules affecting the business of people who sold livestock, those businesses could file a complaint and were entitled to a hearing with the Secretary of Agriculture. In the case, the business had already done this, but then they went to court arguing that the hearing had not been fair. They said this violated the statute and their 5th Amendment right to an opportunity to be heard. The 5th Amendment restrains the federal government; the 14th Amendment restrains the State government. The Court said it didn't have to get into the 5th Amendment argument, because the wording of the statute already said the businesses were entitled to a "full hearing." The Court said that under the statute a hearing in front of the Secretary was supposed to be like a hearing in court in front of a judge. The Court then broke down what that means.

BOOG: *I'm looking at pages 480 and 481. And it says,*

...There must be a full hearing. There must be evidence adequate to support pertinent and necessary findings of fact. Nothing can be treated as evidence which is not introduced as such...Facts and circumstances which ought be considered must not be excluded. Facts and circumstances must not be considered which should not legally influence the conclusion. Findings based on the evidence must embrace the basic facts which are needed to sustain the order. NEXT PAGE ... A proceeding of this sort requiring the taking and weighing of evidence, determinations of fact based upon the consideration of the evidence and the making of an order supported by such findings, has a quality resembling that of a JUDICIAL PROCEEDING....The requirement of a "full hearing" has obvious reference to THE TRADITION OF JUDICIAL PROCEEDINGS in which evidence is received and weighed by the trier of facts...The HEARING is the hearing of EVIDENCE AND ARGUMENT. If the one who determines the facts which underlie the order had not considered evidence or argument....THE HEARING HAS NOT BEEN GIVEN.

BK: In that last sentence, the Court tells us that if the judge ignores our evidence and argument when he or she made the decision, then we just got burnt out of our hearing. The hearing has not been given. That's been happening to me for 25 years. And thousands upon thousands of prisoners can tell you the same thing. JUSTICE means a decision based on evidence, facts, the TRUTH. This is not a system of justice, and it never will be until we really get that most basic right—the opportunity to be heard!

BOOG: *Excellence!*

BK: My pleasure, Boog.

BOOG: *Last words for the youth, who can possibly be saved from this madness?*

BK: Go drive trucks! Of all the things I could say, right? I'm serious though. A lot of dudes are coming out of prison and becoming truck drivers, making decent loot, buying homes and cars, etc. And the news just said there's a shortage. Hopefully, the young cats will wise up and do it before they end up in prison. Go drive trucks.

BOOG: *That was the first of a series of necessary interviews that will appear in this opus designed to inspire and to ignite the desire for change. If I can change, anyone can.*

But before we end, it must also be noted that the Due Process Clause of the Fourteenth Amendment, "protects the accused against conviction except upon proof beyond a reasonable doubt of every fact necessary to constitute the crime with which he is charged." In re Winship, 397 U.S. 358, 364, 90 S.Ct. 1068, 25 L.Ed.2d 368 (1970).

Chapter Eight
The Purpose of The Act...

The Purpose of The Act...

The stated purpose of the Pennsylvania POST CONVICTION RELIEF ACT (PCRA) is to offer relief to those convicted. See 42 Pa. C.S.A. §9542 which reads, ("This subchapter provides for action by which persons convicted of crimes they did not commit and persons serving illegal sentences may obtain collateral relief.") *Com. v. Morris*, 565 Pa. 1, 32, 771 A.2d 721, 739 (Pa. 2001) ("this Court called for legislation governing collateral proceedings in order to afford "an adequate corrective process for hearing and determining" alleged constitutional violations... [t]he purpose [ ] was to provide a procedure which encompassed habeas corpus and corum nobia and to decide challenges to convictions that were imposed without due process.")

That sounds clear and concise, with some true guidance, but the PCRA is maybe one of the most complicated things I've ever had to learn. Just when I think I have figured it out I get an opinion that contradicts and confuses as though they are making things up as they go.

To be eligible for relief under the PCRAs a Petitioner must plead and prove by a preponderance of the evidence that his convictions or sentence resulted from one or more of the circumstances enumerated in Title 42 Pa. C.S.A. §9543.

These circumstances include:

(a) that the Petitioner has been convicted of a crime under the laws of this Commonwealth and is at the time relief is granted:

(i) currently serving a sentence of imprisonment, ... for the crime.

(b) that the conviction or sentence resulted from one of more of the following:

(i) a violation of the Constitution of the Commonwealth or the Constitution or law of the United States, which in the circumstances of the particular case so undermined the truthdetermining process that no reliable adjudication of guilt or innocence could have taken place.

(ii) ineffective assistance of counsel which, in the circumstances of the particular case, so undermined the truth determining process that no reliable adjudication of guilt or innocence could have taken place.

(vi) the unavailability at the time of trial of exculpatory evidence that has subsequently become available and could have changed the outcome of the trial if it had been introduced.

(c) that the allegations of error has not been previously litigated or waived. §9544.

(d) the failure to litigate the[se] issue(s) prior to or during trial,...or on direct appeal could not have been the result of any rational, strategic, or tactical decision by counsel. Title

42 Pa. C.S. §9543.

All of the above is easier said than done.

Over the course of my 24 years of incarceration, I've filed 4 PCRA Petitions on my own. Pro Se! which means without legal counsel. If I didn't do it, no one would.

I've cited newly discovered evidence, governmental interference, prosecutorial misconduct, ineffective assistance of counsel. I've brought it all. And as I've stated previously, even when I knew I was in over my head, I gave it my all. Unfortunately, I was unsuccessful. But my unfinished business (*that's what I call it*), not failures, wasn't the result of something I was doing wrong. The PCRA is laden with restrictions, and so much deference is given to the judges who oversee these Petitions. A lot of the times they get it wrong. And all the time, they also appoint incompetent attorneys, whom themselves exude a lack of concern.

In this part of the book, I thought it would be dope to really get to the bottom of the PCRA, and its true intent.

*****

Sam Ross, my friend and brother from another mother, has one of the sharpest legal minds I have encountered behind the G-wall.

BOOG: *Sam Ross, where do we start? Tell the people where you are from...*

SAM ROSS: I'm from Erie Ave. The city inside the city.

Inside of North Philly.

BOOG: *And when was the last time you were on Erie Ave.?*

SR: May 1996. That was the last time I've seen Philly.

BOOG: *I recognized you as many things. A solid dude, a good advisor, genuine, and the owner of a great legal mind. How long did it take for you to learn the law?*

SR: About three years after I exhausted all my remedies in Federal Court. That's when the jail-house legal help stopped.

BOOG: *So, someone was helping you? Is that what you mean when you say the jail-house legal help stopped?*

SR: Exactly. But my fight for freedom was still ignited. I could never adapt to being in prison. I made my adjustments, but never adapted.

BOOG: *I can relate.*

SR: In making adjustments, I attended the law library faithfully, learning how to read and research case law.

BOOG: *Is that how you became sharp? Because I have an unconditional relationship with the law library too.*

SR: What really helped me become sharp with the law was when I began studying Free Masonry.

BOOG: *Interesting...*

SR: Back then, we all used to hear the stories of judges and lawyers being masons; of how a lawyer would do certain hand signals and get a defendant off scott free.

BOOG: *So, you started studying Free Masonry?*

SR: Yeah. To learn them hand signals. And to learn how judges think.

BOOG: *Did you ever learn the hand signs?*

SR: Never learned them. But I did learn the importance of having a free mind, and the three eternal enemies of a free mind, which are: ignorance, fanaticism, and tyranny.

BOOG: *Interesting...keep...going.*

SR: Out of the three one stood out the most, fanaticism, because being a fanatic means you are marked with intense uncritical devotion.

BOOG: *And that helped you how?*

SR: I began to criticize every move I made after that.

BOOG: *In regard to the law?*

SR: Instead of researching case law that supported my arguments, I began to research case law to learn how the courts was getting around my arguments. Instead of taking court rulings for face value, I began to study the origins of law. That's when I really learned the law.

BOOG: *We're here to discuss critical law as it pertains to post conviction. So, I have to ask. How many PCRA's have you filed over your twenty-five years of incarceration?*

SR: About thirteen. One was a State Habeas turned into a PCRA by the Superior Court. And one was an Application for Relief under the PA Constitution, Article I, Section 11,

"Remedies Clause," which was also converted to a PCRA.

BOOG: *So, do you feel like you were getting a fair shake in the courts when making your collateral attacks on your conviction?*

SR: Absolutely not! First of all, my first PCRA should've never been dismissed because neither the appointed attorney, nor the judge had litigated my appellate counsel Ineffectiveness claim.

BOOG: *Elaborate.*

SR: I was ambushed in one day by appointed counsel filing a nomerit letter, and the judge dismissing the PCRA without giving the mandatory 20-day Notice of Intent to Dismiss.

BOOG: *The 907 Notice?*

SR: Right! In one day, I was without legal representation, and had thirty days to appeal.

BOOG: *You didn't even know how to file appeals yet?*

SR: Right. To make matters worse, the court never gave its independent reasoning for dismissal of my PCRA. So, I didn't even know what to appeal.

BOOG: *That's heavy. I can relate.*

SR: All of my PCRA's, with the exception of one, was attempts to have the appellate counsel Ineffectiveness Claim heard and decided in accordance with the law. Despite the claim having already defeated the time-bar, the courts kept dismissing my PCRA's as untimely. And the Superior Court played the role of Big Brother to the lower court, or even worse, as a secondary PCRA court.

BOOG: *July 21, 2003, I had some new evidence, and I was just learning the law myself, and I filed an Application for Remand. The Superior Court, on August 29, 2003, dismissed my motion, but ruled that I could argue the motel records claim in my upcoming brief. However, an administrative mix-up ensued. The Superior Court FORGOT about the application, and on May 11, 2004, dismissed the motel records claim as waived. I remember it like it was yesterday, and that was seventeen years ago.*

SR: I've witnessed the Superior Court oust facts, create false facts, etc., to prevent from giving me the relief I was entitled to. Real talk, once you get to the collateral attack stages, the laws become foreign language to the courts here in Pennsylvania.

BOOG: *Tell the readers why appellate counsel was ineffective, then we will get into your perception of the PCRA.*

SR: I raised appellate counsel's ineffectiveness as issue three. To withdraw as counsel, the law requires counsel to list and explain why each claim lacks merit. I raised six issues, PCRA counsel made it appear as though he was addressing issues 1, 2 and 3 in one single paragraph. He only addressed the first two, avoiding number three.

BOOG: *Okay, then what?*

SR: The court unlawfully permitted PCRA counsel to withdraw and unlawfully relied solely on PCRA counsel's No-Merit letter.

BOOG: *To dismiss the petition.*

SR: Right. Never ever addressing the ineffective claim. The law was completely absent from my first PCRA matter and contrary to achieving finality.

BOOG: *FINALITY is a very powerful world, with devastating impact. The legislative intent was by design to slam the door shut on convicted individuals. Better known as the Time-Bar. A last-minute addition to the AEDPA, signed into law the spring of 1996 by Bill Clinton.*

SR: Right. The only achievement though was denying me the right to effective PCRA counsel and to the right to have the right to file a Petition for Allowance of Appeal to the PA Supreme Court on direct appeal.

BOOG: *You were challenging your sentence though, not a trial error?*

SR: Right. I got 30 to 60 years. And no guidelines were considered. No reason was provided for why the Judge deviated from the aggravated ranges by an additional 13 years.

BOOG: *So, by law, you were supposed to get seventeen years?*

SR: Right. On Post-Sentence Motions counsel did raise

legal arguments, like the courts not considering the guidelines. He cited the law that mandated the courts to do these things.

BOOG: *You got a hearing on that, right?*

SR: Yes. The judge not only indicated that he considered the wrong guidelines, but he also made an improper guideline calculation when he cited ranges that never existed in PA. And, on appeal the attorney abandoned the legal argument for a discretionary one.

BOOG: *Explain that Bro.*

SR: Legal arguments bind the Appellate Court to interpret and apply the law, while discretionary arguments do not, and the Appellate Court can rule on your claims without the law. Also, with legal questions you have the right to appeal up to the Supreme Court. Discretionary questions stop at the Superior Court, but with the right to appeal a misapplication of law to the Supreme Court.

BOOG: *Did you make it to the State Supreme Court?*

SR: On appeal, the Superior Court declined to review the excessive and unreasonable sentence issue because the sentences were within statutory limits.

BOOG: *I know this because I been jailing with you. But tell the people how they came to such a conclusion that this was justice.*

SR: Superior Court affirmed the 30 to 60 without looking to the guidelines to determine whether the sentences were excessive and without reviewing the excessive sentence for unreasonableness as the law mandates.

BOOG: *Now we are looping back around. This is where counsel failed you.*

SR: I get two letters stating he would file an appeal with the Supreme Court. Then he sends me a letter ending his representation, telling me I didn't have a right to appeal the discretionary aspects of sentencing to the Supreme Court. He presented this to me as if he had just found out this law himself. But now that I know law, he had that set up the moment he abandoned my legal based claims on appeal. I respond to his mail and request that he still file. He responds on the day of the deadline and says he's not doing it, clearly depriving me the right to effective assistance of counsel on appeal, the right to appeal preserved legal claims, and the right to file an appeal to the Supreme Court of PA.

BOOG: *I get it, and I'm sure the people will too. That is why you filed, in your timely first PCRA his ineffectiveness?*

SR: You already know.

BOOG: *The system is flawed, deeply flawed. That's why I wanted to write this book. Because still we rise... Here is Sam Ross' perspective of the PCRA... It may not be what you want to hear, but it is what it is. And quite frankly, the PCRA is in need of not just a facelift, but reconstructive surgery.*

SR: My perception of the PCRA (Post Conviction Relief

Act) is it is a ‘lock them up and throw away the key’ method. The PCRA’s time-bar is the ‘throw away the key’ equivalent.

In 1995, the PCRA was amended, and a one-year jurisdictional limitation was added. The Courts interpreted the jurisdictional limitation as a scheme in which PCRA petitions are to be accorded finality. However, the deception that one can only view through the lens of common sense indicates a scheme to close the door of the Courts on the rights of a prisoner and to deny him or her justice.

Common Sense view #1:

A prisoner, who more than likely has maybe a 10th grade or less ‘public school’ education, is forced with the hardship of learning and applying the law in one year that takes a lawyer about 7 years to learn and apply. That immediately puts the prisoner at a disadvantage against that Commonwealth who has learned and been applying the law for decades.

Common Sense view #2:

To hold that the one-year jurisdictional limitation is constitutional, the State Supreme Court deceptively cited a partial legal reasoning from a very old case from 1879 (Sayers v. Commonwealth, 88 Pa. 291) regarding the constitutionality of a statute of limitation. Relying on the legal reasoning for a statute of limitation to support why a jurisdictional limitation is constitutional is the equivalent of using a football helmet to explain why a baseball helmet is safe. A statute of limitation can be equitably tolled, and the Courts remain open for the correction of constitutional violations. A jurisdictional limitation closes the door of the Courts and has tolerated constitutional violations upon constitutional violations at the alter of finality. However, the constitution does not sanction such tolerance and rather provides that State Constitutional rights are forever inviolate (Pa. Const. Art. I, §25) and the United States Constitutional rights are Supreme Law of the land and anything in the Constitution or laws of any state to the contrary notwithstanding (U.S. Const. Art. 6, Cl. 2 - Supremacy Clause). If you read the Sayers case, it goes on to state that if for any sufficient reason the time has been allowed to pass, any one of the justices of this court has the power to allow the writ. It would be his clear duty to do so if the case presented any merits. That's on page 309. Deceptively, the Court did not cite that part, but only referred to page 307. See: *Com. v. Peterkin*, 722 A.2d 638, page 642. (1998). It was that portion of legal reasoning that made the statute of limitation discussed in Sayers constitutional because it denied no man's right and it imposed no hardship upon any defendant. The PCRA jurisdictional limitation clearly denies the right to access to the court and the right to constitutional protection in the face of the Supremacy Clause and the State Constitution's reservation of powers in People.

Common Sense view #3:

The Court will appoint you a lawyer. That right to a lawyer on a PCRA is a rule-based right, not a constitutional right. So, the lawyer can misrepresent you, deny you the helping legal hand and not violate the constitution. The lawyer, once appointed, has two options. One, he can amend the pro se PCRA petition the prisoner has filed without legal knowledge or, two, he can file a no-merit letter to argue that your issues lack merit. Either way, the lawyer gets paid. Majority of the time, the lawyer will file the no-merit letter because then he will only have to argue against issues raised by the prisoner who is ignorant of the law. To amend will require the lawyer to actually do lawyer work like reading transcripts, investigating, viewing document, etc., to look for issues to be raised in an amended petition. When the Court permits the lawyer to withdraw, the prisoner is left to fight for himself or herself without the knowledge of how to litigate or what to litigate on appeal. However, if the prisoner does have knowledge of the law and seeks to waive the lawyer's representation the Court suddenly has concern about whether the prisoner understands his rights and whether he or she knows they are still bound by all normal procedural rules and that potential claims may be permanently lost if not timely asserted. If the Court feels that you are not knowledged in law to represent yourself, they will force you to have appointed representation. But, when it comes to the Courts being aware that you are ignorant of the law and the appointed lawyer seeks to withdraw because the prisoner could not do lawyer work, the Court has no concern about the prisoner's rights nor about what potential claims may be lost. Surely, the court is not going to read any transcripts or documents to determine whether there were any issues to be raised. It is all a deception. A fallacy of appointing you a lawyer.

Common Sense view #4:

Prior to the amendment of the one-year jurisdictional limitation, a prisoner could file unlimited PCHA petitions alleging errors in his trial, so long as he alleged that each prior counsel was ineffective. Under the PCRA, you have to learn of trial court errors, of ineffectiveness of counsel, of the law to apply to them errors, all within one year to raise ineffective counsel. Mind you, that is with no knowledge of the law. In case you do not learn this in time, you will not be able to raise ineffective counsel later and to be sure of that, the general assembly made it clear that defense counsel, whether appointed or retained, is not included as a government official. This is how you see the deception. If the Government appoints you a lawyer, the Government is paying the lawyer, then the lawyer is without a doubt an officer of the Court, a government official.

Common Sense view #5:

The PCRA has three exceptions to the jurisdictional

limitation.

(1) Government Interference, (2) After-discovered Evidence, and (3) New Recognized Constitutional Right. In regard to government interference, which counsel is not included as such, the exception itself is a joke because nothing falls under government interference. Unless the Court itself makes a mistake and erroneously gives you false information, the exception has no play. In regard to the After-Discovered Evidence exception, that is the one valid exception depending upon the evidence. In regard to the Newly Recognized Constitutional Right exception, that is a joke as well because the statute states that the Court that made the ruling has to have held the ruling to be retroactive before the prisoner can apply for the exception. This is a joke simply because 99% of the time, neither the United States Supreme Court nor the State Supreme Court will express whether the ruling is retroactive or not. In applying common sense, a constitutional right should be retroactive because the constitution itself is not new, the ruling itself was just late. Actually, the ruling is saying that the Courts who previously viewed such issue was not enforcing the constitution correctly. So, the judges, entrusted to enforce the law, can be ignorant of the law, but ignorance of the law is no excuse when it comes to a prisoner. Another thing, in applying common sense, the Court who made the newly

recognized constitutional ruling should express in that case whether it will be retroactive or not. It only takes one sentence! This ruling is retroactive, or this ruling will not be retroactive. The Courts are aware of the statute's requirement that the new ruling be held retroactive, but rather it keeps things complicated. It keeps the law complicated so the prisoner, ignorant of the law, will have a hard time learning and applying the law in a court who has as much respect for the law than the person accused of violating the law.

It is all deception and anyone who looks at the P CRA with common sense will be enlightened to the hypocrisy, the contradictions, and the intent to "lock them up" and elude them in the courts until they are time-barred, which is equivalent of 'throwing away the key'.

BOOG: *Thank you, bro. I knew you would come with the goods. That's why I asked you to join me, have a seat, you dig. In my estimation, you have become more than they expected. You didn't let the time do you, you did the time.*

SR: (heartfelt laughter...)

BOOG: *Any words for the youth, Sam Ross???*

SR: Thank you for having me, Bro.

BOOG: *My pleasure.*

SR: So, my message to the youth. Stop chasing death! Live your life! Living is about enjoying the company of your family and friends, about doing what you love, about succeeding and being comfortable. If you're not living life, you're living a slow death. When you pick up that gun and you got murder in your heart, you are living a slow death. Death will come way too early for y'all. Death is death. Ain't no coming back for a second chance to live a better life or to do things different. It's a wrap. A life sentence in prison is a slow death. It's best to do life living life as a free and happy man, a free and happy kid, than to spend twenty-plus years fighting for a life you could have lived. Live life, have fun.

BOOG: *I've spent twenty-plus years fighting the courts. It's not fun. In fact, it's very taxing.*

Before we close out, I have to add: the design of this literary piece is not just for me to tell my horror story, but also about delivering the goods and from a journalistic approach. Any good journalist worth half his or her name leaves no stone unturned.

After further research and phone conversations with two of my comrades, both having been convicted of first-degree murder before eventual exonerations here in the Commonwealth of Pennsylvania—Lorenz "Cat" Johnson (*life sentence*) and Roddy "Demon" Johnson (*death sentence*)—it is verified that 9545(b) (1)(i) Government interference (an exception to the PCRA time bar) is viable for the foul acts of government officials. (Prosecutors, police, etc.)

In Cat and Demon's wrongful convictions the government

withheld information favorable to both defendants, (separate cities, separate cases). Under 9545(b)(1)(i), "the petitioner must plead and prove that the failure to previously raise these claims was the result of interference by government officials, and that the information could not have been obtained earlier with the exercise of due diligence." *Com. v. Smith*, 2018 PA Super 211, 194 A.3d 126, 133 (Pa. Super. 2018).

Prosecutors are government officials. Cat was released from prison July 2017 after serving 22 years. Demon was released December 2020 after spending 22 years on death row. They are both back in New York liberated and living their best lives.

It could happen to any of us, *the good, the bad and the ugly*.

Chapter Nine
Commutation in Pennsylvania

Commutation in Pennsylvania

In 2019, I was offered the opportunity to blog for the Justice For Youth Foundation. That's where my opportunity to write perspective pieces really got its legs. One of the topics was commutation, and the carelessness of government when it comes to clemency applications where men and women have served lengthy periods of time and have placed themselves at the mercy of the government hoping for a second chance.

I've been incarcerated unjustly for 24 years and counting. But the gentleman I've chosen to sit down with happen to be one of Pennsylvania's longest standing LIFERS. Mr. Russell Sewell, AC-9731, has served 53 years.

I salute this brother, as he has demonstrated exemplary discipline in the decade-plus that I have known and known of him. And, under harsh circumstances. *Greeting, Mr. Russell.*

RUSSELL SEWELL: Good morning.

BOOG: *When I asked you to do this, I wasn't certain what your response would be. When you agreed, I immediately felt like my imagination is still my closest comrade.*

RS: Let's do it.

BOOG: *The first thing I want to know is, how old were you when you started this bid?*

RS: I had just turned eighteen. I wasn't even eighteen for a week. I must stress that point because had I been seventeen,

I would have fit under the resentencing of juvenile lifers' laws. I was eighteen in age, but the last grade I completed was the 6th. I would be free right now, with time served. Commutation would not even be necessary.

BOOG: *Wow. That's crazy. But there are criminal justice reform organizations pushing to have the definition of juvenile expanded, based on science, of course, from seventeen and under to 18-24. Mr. Russell, what year was that?*

RS: 1968. It was a year of turmoil.

BOOG: *The year Dr. King was assassinated.*

RS: Yes! And the country was in turmoil. I got swept up in the wave of crime as a young person with very little education. I was into stealing cars, and that's where I got the gun which inevitably became the weapon used in my crime. My first crime and conviction. In the 60's, stealing cars was how we passed time. That was what we considered "wilding out" as the young kids say today.

BOOG: *How much have you changed since the days of wilding out?*

RS: Not only have I became an adult, but I became an old man. I understand life, and I really understand my mistake. And I prefer to call it a mistake rather than a crime because I know it was a mistake. 50 seconds has resulted in a life being taken, and me spending 53 years. Been so long in here I stopped counting the years.

BOOG: *Fifty-three years straight.*

RS: I escaped in 1972. They brought me back in 1976. Had I not taken that chance, I would not have my three children. Yet and still, I have regrets about that.

BOOG: *How much has prison changed since you first came in?*

RS: There was no appliances. No TV's and radios in the cell. LIFERS went home. Oh, no double cells.

BOOG: *No double bunking???*

RS: Nope. Prison wasn't big business back then. And everybody went home.

BOOG: *LIFERS too?*

RS: Yes. After fifteen years. Back then commutation actually was functioning. But now they don't let people go. Because it's big business.

BOOG: *H ow many appeals have you filed over the years?*

RS: At least five. I had five court-appointed lawyers, and never met one of them face to face.

BOOG: *Not one of them? Sounds so familiar. I can relate. And I go in depth about lawyers in this book. But go ahead, finish your thought.*

RS: If I had a lawyer, my life might be different.

BOOG: *When was the last time you had a write-up?*

RS: Let me see. (Mr. Russell takes time to think.) State Prison Huntingdon, dirty urine, twenty years ago. And I never smoked another joint.

BOOG: *There has been a lot of media coverage surrounding commutation in Pennsylvania. And, like never before. So, I have to ask, when you think of commutation, what is the first thing that comes to mind?*

RS: No faith. I just been watching and listening to people with cleaner jail records than me being denied the chance to rejoin their loved ones. LIFERS once used this—the 7O's and 8O's—and it was good business. Then that went away.

BOOG: *There was a situation in Pennsylvania in the 9O's, and I'm quite sure you will know exactly what I'm talking about when you hear the name, because it effected people for decades. Does MudMan ring a bell?*

RS: Mud-Man was an excuse. They knew what kind of guy he was. They knew him. If the prisoners know a person is no good, then administration knows too! They know even more than the prisoners. Still, he was granted commutation. And today we are still suffering for his mess.

BOOG: *So, you're saying, had he not been commuted, things would be different?*

RS: Greatly! They wanted it this way, because you don't have to punish everybody because of one person. Unless you want to. Because they know everyone's not like him. (Mud-Man was commuted, then killed a cop in New Jersey).

BOGG: *Have you filed for commutation under the Wolf*

Administration's adaptation of the commutation process?

RS: Yes. And only because guys here convinced me to do it. I have no faith in it at all. Because even now, you need five votes to get to the governor's desk. The process is rough. In the 7O's it was just an easy flow. A steady flow. They were interested in getting LIFERS out. Once it gets clogged up, you can't fix it. Because before, no one was watching. It wasn't so publicized.

BOOG: *How many times did you file before that?*

RS: This is my first time. I was hoping for them to expand the age of juvenile LIFERS from seventeen to 18-24. Then I would benefit from that criterion. Most of the LIFERS in Pennsylvania would. But my commutation is filed right now. Let's see what happens.

BOOG: *Is there anything you would like to say to the youth?*

RS: Be careful. Because, in the blink of an eye, it took 50 seconds to make this mistake and cost me 50 years. And I shot a guy in the arm. He passed from that injury. I only pulled the trigger because I was scared...the guy I was robbing knew me.

BOOG: *I appreciate you giving me the opportunity to sit down with you to discuss such a serious topic, being as commutation is the only release valve for 5,600 LIFERS imprisoned in Pennsylvania, unless you were under 18 when the offense was committed, or the sentence is vacated.*

What is most remarkable is, just two states away, my home state, The Empire State, with good time, and after serving 20 years on a LIFE sentence, you can be released through the parole board.

It is my hope that one day, LIFE means in Pennsylvania what it means in other states. A second chance. Thank you, Mr. Russell. I'm rooting for you, and all LIFERS.

RS: You're welcome. And thank you, Boogie.

BOOG: I appreciate you giving me some of your precious time.

Here's where we get into the numbers.

According to a recent study, in Pennsylvania where I have been incarcerated my entire adult life, Black people make up only 12 percent of the population, but we make up 65 percent of prisoners serving Death By Incarceration sentences. That means either an African-American woman or man has been convicted of First-Degree Murder, or Felony Murder.

That is a staggering number and is not just a coincidence. These numbers represent a problem within the justice system and should disturb anyone with a conscience.

There is roughly 2.3 million people convicted in the United States. Approximately 5 percent of those prisoners are believed to be innocent or wrongly convicted. That is about 115,000 people suffering at the hands of immoral prosecutors.

Sadly, there just aren't enough Innocence Projects, not

enough Civil Rights Attorneys, not enough funding, and far too many prosecutors uninterested in justice, and unwilling to admit they made a mistake.

In a June 27, 2021, Philadelphia Daily News article, a United States Judge was quoted as saying:

"The responsibility of doing justice does not disappear once a conviction is achieved. In some circumstances, the duty to seek truth can and should extend to cases long closed."

I truly believe that these numbers (65% of prisoners serving LIFE in Pennsylvania are African-American while we only make up 12 percent of the state's population) and realities (115,000 innocent or wrongly convicted in the U.S.) disturbed LT. Governor Fetterman, and maybe even encouraged his sudden but necessary Mercy Mission.

In an unprecedented move, LT. Governor Fetterman did a series of interviews via media, print, and online media, local and regional, and even visited a state prison, encouraging prisoners with decades served to file for commutation, ensuring that things would be different than they had been in the past 20 years. One thing that was surely different, the Lieutenant Governor had hired a black man with a criminal past as the Secretary of the Board of Pardons. I recall bringing my hands together in a congratulatory clap when Brandon Flood took his place in history as the first black man to hold the position.

I have spent significant time in the Restricted Housing Unit (the hole) for everything from fist fights to unauthorized use of a cellphone, yet Fetterman's message was so compelling that my application for commutation was on the verge of completion. I thought that even a convict like myself could prosper and be freed from my wrongful conviction, clemency serving as the release valve. My imagination even allowed for the idea that this process wasn't the Boogie Man, and that this liberation outlet was a newly oiled machine that wasn't lubricated with snake oil.

For many, commutation is the only reprieve from a Death sentence by Incarceration. And many will desperately venture into this process knowing that we could very well be being set up for abundant disappointment. *That is the very definition of hope*. Never relinquish the hope of a better day.

Mr. Russell has expressed the very reason why we should hope for the best but expect the worst when it comes to Pennsylvania's commutation process.

There are House Bills, and Senate Bills being drafted and floated throughout the chambers of PA's congress in hopes of reducing the necessary unanimous vote of 5 to that of 4 to be commuted. I'd even read an article where progressive lawmakers are pushing for a 3 of the 5 Board members to give a favorable nod and a prisoner's request of mercy can make it to the governor's desk for his stamp of approval.

However, when it comes to criminal justice reform (*with the exception of the great work being done in the Philadelphia District Attorney's Office*), Pennsylvania is the last state to implement true change.

Between May 2018 and May 2021, 21 people have been exonerated in Philadelphia. Three of which I know personally: John "Littles" Miller (*22 years served*), Johnny "Nose" Berry (*25 years served*), and Dontai "Tay" Patterson (*11 years served*). All three of these men were serving LIFE sentences for crimes they were innocent of.

To believe that Philadelphia is the only county in Pennsylvania with malicious prosecutors and corrupt cops is to say, "slavery was a choice." *And we all know that was not the case.*

My favorite lyricist of all time, Nasir Jones, put out a smash hit the summer of 1996. It's called *If I Ruled The World.*

I won't go that far: *Imagining I ruled the world.*

However, if I had *One Wish* like Ray J., it would be that in Pennsylvania, LIFERS receive parole after 25 years.

I believe that parole for LIFERS would bring the Keystone State into the future, and give the men and women incentive, something to strive for, while also eliminating the possibility of men and women dying in prison for crimes they hadn't committed. As well as freeing from captivity prisoners who have been redeemed and rehabilitated and are more than capable of contributing to society.

At the time of me writing this book, and since Fetterman's announcement of change spring 2019, only one LIFER has been commuted here at Somerset. Dozens and dozens and dozens are awaiting. God Bless the LIFERS, because many have been denied without explanation.

I close this part of the book acknowledging that more prisoners have been commuted in the last 2 years than there has been in the previous 20 years. And that is progress, but there is still much work that must be done.

Epilogue

Epilogue

My toughest challenge as a writer has been here and now. I had to explain to readers how I survived 24 years of a wrongful conviction without losing my mind? *It was not easy*. How I managed to stay relevant? *That was hard.* How I was able to stay in court, and keep getting hearings? *That was hard work.* How I was able to attract the support of people who could help me realize my visions? *No longer was I afraid of being vulnerable.* How I became a prolific writer? Hard work. And how I landed my Legal Dream Team? *Now that, I don't have one specific answer for*. But I will say this: when people think they have nothing to live for, they behave like they have nothing to live for, thus that will be how people treat you.

When I probably wasn't supposed to, I've figured out how to turn a negative into a positive. And that is how *It Can Happen To Any Of Us* truly came about.

I do not have a degree in law. I did not acquire a degree in social work. I am not a graduate of political science. I did not go to school for journalism. However, I am an expert by experience. I immersed myself in what I wanted to learn, what I needed to know, and that is very important for anyone who is truly interested in elevating.

Now although, I've listed my credentials in the Foreword,

I felt I need to mention the above because throughout this book, I've discussed law, politics and policy, as well as social status. All of which I have spent much time entertaining during the course of my incarceration. Bottom line, knowledge is power. And maturity is not solely connected to age, but experience more than anything.

I truly believe I did not suffer all those years just because. My troubles, my travels, my triumphs are meant to be shared.

Now, all life sentences are not equal. Pennsylvania is one of 6 states that doesn't allow for its lifers to see parole. Here in PA, one can receive life for 2nd Degree if someone dies in the commission of another crime (arson, rape or robbery). However, I believe there is more to it than just that, (I'm not talking the differentiation between First- and Second-Degree Murder.) *What do I mean by that?* All First-Degree Murders are not First-degree murders. I believe, some of the people serving life are not guilty of First, but because of far reach, and stretches of the imagination by prosecutors, there are more people serving life than there should be. For instance, more than two-thirds of PA's lifer population are co-defendants, not the person who actually took the life.

To give a young Black or minority a life sentence is to some prosecutors trophy pieces. Accolades for their mantles. Almost as if they're competing—*who can give out the most life sentences????*

Think of Cassanova and the Gentleman Caller of the James Patterson's thriller, *Kiss the Girls*. Those two guys were the least suspected of doing dirt because they fit the part of what societal norms reflect. And that allowed for them to imprison women, or straight take their lives. Prosecutors who cheat are no different than those fictitious characters.

I've talked about my past—*seven to eight years in the streets before my arrest in January 1998*. When I was drug dealing, state to state.

Some consider drug dealing to be genocide. But there's a case to be made that you can't lead a revolution through good deeds alone. And rising up out of poverty is a revolution I was a part of in the 90's.

See, my mother had nothing, and her mother had nothing, and there was an urgency to break that cycle of having nothing. While being broke is temporary and not necessarily embedded into one's psyche, poverty is a whole other animal. I grew up poor, and that is a condition that could become permanent dependent upon one's ability and ambitions.

Sadly, I didn't have to watch mafia movies to see ruthlessness, to see brutality, to witness treachery. Organized crime was right outside my bedroom window. Directly in front of my building. Right before my naive eyes, crime bosses, their underbosses and the block boss were prospering off crack.

There in that neighborhood we weren't raised with

middle class values or upper crust creed. We were raised at the bottom, taught to police ourselves. So personal growth, personal success, empowerment—those values got picked up on the streets. That is why I call myself a street dude. And a real street dude is not letting anyone take anything from them. *That includes the taking of freedom unjustly.*

Just as we encounter haters who wish one the worst, there are the rare occasions when I would run across a young don (*a younger dude possessing admirable traits reminiscent of the golden era*) who would abruptly state, "*Damn, OG, I ain't know you had wheels. I hope you shake back. We need OG's like you out there.*" It would truly be a shocker to the young don when someone just puts my business out there (revealed my sanction and sentence wittingly or unwittingly).

Like I'd stated early on in this book, early on in my incarceration, I hid my sentence. But you know what moments like such would make me more ambitious. Moments like that would reinforce my mentality. I had a vibe that would not allow for me to be dirtied by the muddy waters. I didn't move like I was wearing cinder blocks for shoes. I didn't allow the dark cloud to float above my head and dump rain on my rally. I moved like the chrome BBS rims were still spinning on my black Acura Coupe. I always kept my appearance up, my mind sharp, my body ready for whatever could come my way. I refused to view this as the end, but instead saw it as the beginning of a supreme challenge. The greatest feeling in the world is doing something no one thinks you can.

To the contrary, I had a few homies who did wear their wheel (*life sentence*) as if it was a badge of honor. As if the calamity had made us inheritants of jail cells, or landlords of cell blocks.

And I understand the mentality of—*gotta make the best of a situation.*

That brings me to one of my favorite quotes by Booker T. Washington:

"The circumstances that surround a man's life are not important. How that man responds to those circumstances is important. His response is the ultimate determining factor between success and failure."

After reading that many years ago, I always felt like there is a better message that could be sent by promoting possibility and having hope versus running things in jail.

I have no qualms with admitting that writing saved me from myself. I take pride in stating the obvious: writing saved my life. The craft taught me immense discipline.

To be a productive writer one must have great discipline and purpose in order to finish what he or she has started. In prison, there are many distractions, and very little to pull inspiration from. So, it is easy to lose focus. Easy to become discouraged. Programs are limited and usually off limits for long-term offenders. For a lifer to have a trade or a worthy skill would appear to be a waste of taxpayers' dollars. At least that's the way it appeared. So, every academic success, every program I completed, I had to campaign for. And once I was in them classes, those programs, I always made it count.

Once on my feet, I always reached back to pull another brother up. A lot of dudes believe I'm intelligent, smart, even intellectual. I've heard it a dozen times. And I rather carry those attributes any day over being deemed: *crazy, wild, reckless, a beast.* Because being the latter ain't convincing no one with some sway to put their name on the line for you. But I think of myself as an instinctual person. I gotta feel it. The greats have that trait to their credit and their success. *Instinct.*

My writing gave me a voice much more powerful and unique than the one I had when I was running the streets, shot calling. This voice is driven by purpose, passion and principles.

My novels weren't written to glorify the streets, my novels were written as cautionary tales. They all end tragically.

In addition to writing several novels, short stories, pieces and articles, I have written many motions, many legal briefs, petitions and memorandums of law. I have not only written for myself, but I have also drafted legal arguments for others resulting in hearings. Mostly post-conviction litigations. I have consulted with dudes leading up to court dates as well.

Here are some writing tips for those looking to get their

manuscripts going.

10 TIPS for WRITING YOUR WAY TO SUCCESS

(1) Create a style, a rhythm, a flow best suited for the way you want to tell your story.

(2) Create time to write daily. Always keep pen and paper on hand.

(3) Never be afraid to make a mess, meaning (only the final draft should you be chasing perfection).

(4) Write at least three drafts (not every word, every sentence, paragraph—but the project as a whole)—because each time you do, a new dimension emerges.

(5) Study other writers; study the craft. I learned how to write by reading.

(6) Write about what you know, not what you think you know. That's very important (that your audience buys into your knowledge of that specific topic).

(7) Be daring, original, and constantly challenge yourself.

(8) Understand that some days you're going to be a genius and others you're going to be below-average. On those days when things aren't clicking, go back to something you wrote that was genius, and channel that creative energy.

(9) Understand your target audience and give them what they want. That heat, that fire!

(10) Paint pictures! Make the pages your canvas! Make the words pop off the page! You want readers to see that shit

happening! What I mean by that is: SHOWING V. TELLING. And knowing when to use one over the other. DON'T TELL HOW HE PROPOSED; SHOW US HOW HE PROPOSED.

What???

Did he ask her to "marry me" while they were off smooching in a remote corner of a state prison visiting room?

-OR-

Did he lower himself onto one knee while lost in her dreamy gray eyes, a tiny red velvet ring box held close to his hamstring, on a white sand beach, as the fading sunlight disappeared into the azure waters behind them???

*****

Now, to truly identify the adversary breakdown in your case and representation, one must read the trial transcript thoroughly, and not only rely on memory. That is very important to one potentially prevailing on a constitutional violation. You may have to write a brief too.

The proofreading part of brief writing is very crucial. Therefore, when preparing a brief or a PCRA petition (and memorandum of law), always proofread. Not just for typos, or grammar, but to assure citations are accurate. Volume numbers, the referenced pages, and dates being accurate are extremely important. Especially for a Pro Se litigant, which is often the case in wrongful convictions. All errors must be deleted and corrected, before being filed with the clerk of courts.

This legal document should be a reflection of your hard work, the many hours of research, and the astute nature of the writer. Errors can distort the confidence of the judge or judges in the substance of the brief.

A Circuit Judge once wrote:

"...[t]here is a gnawing feeling on occasion that the obviousness of the uncorrected errors indicates that the brief, having not been read for these errors, may be equally unreliable in its substantive reasoning or its analysis of authorities."

Does this mean justice should be denied? No. Absolutely not! But mistakes that are noticeable and missed because of a failure to proofread, can and often will discredit a Pro Se petitioner's position.

Being Pro Se already puts us at a disadvantage.

*****

I study the past and I pay attention to current events so that I can have a future. Once I bought into those principles, my life began to change. Good things began to happen for me. Good people began to come into my life.

Being convicted of a crime you didn't commit is the worst. Being told you are "guilty" is about as enjoyable as falling from the rooftop of a 20-story building. It was a direct hit to my self-confidence and my psyche.

I know what the men and women are going through...

Let's take this selfie! I'm not talking about a pic. I'm 1 talking about *self-love*, *self-respect*, *self-discipline*, *self-knowledge*, and warding off that *self-hate* and *self-destruction*. Time to rebuild that *self-esteem!*

Like any other form of success, overturning a conviction takes discipline, comprehension, sacrifice and hard work. Surround yourself with people who are smarter than you, more successful than you, and who are good for you. Because it takes a team, and it takes convincing that team to ride for you. Not through words, but through your actions and conduct.

Here are four steps to rebuilding that self-confidence.

(1) Envision freedom.

The mind is a powerful thing. The power of visualization is not enough. You must think things into existence. For years, people have fooled the brain into believing success has arrived. What it's going to look like, feel like, and even taste like. Just like, if you believe you are defeated you will be consumed by those thoughts. Of course, you have to put the work in too.

(2) Take a step back and regain your footing.

Affirmation increases confidence, envisioning nothing but positive things, and embracing the challenges before you. You can talk to yourself, just don't talk back. LOL.

(3) Even when you're losing you should be planning a way to win.

Start with small wins, like adding on to your knowledge,

not being afraid to request help, or helping others so you can familiarize yourself with the sensation of progress again. This creates that biofeedback we need to keep from being stagnant, dormant or defeated. When you achieve at something, significant or minute, your body lets off higher levels of testosterone and dopamine that creates the addiction to progression. Greater testosterone levels increase your desire to be victorious. Dopamine is the neurochemical that tells your brain "this is good." It's a natural high you will constantly be chasing.

(4) Never allow your body language to speak for you.

People perceive us by how we carry ourselves, long before they hear us speak. They think they can tell how we feel about ourselves by our body language. Taking on strong body posture, power poses and body carriage that contains confidence, will make you think and feel confident. One of the old adages I live by is, "CONFIDENCE IS KING."

Men, women, family, friends, those steps worked for me.

Today, I feel like prison can no longer contain me, or the level of energy that I have cultivated. I feel like, after 24 years of captivity, I am destined to be liberated. Like, the forces that control fate must accommodate my access to get my message to those in true need. And soon! However, I will never be free of my duties (the call to duty). And what I mean by that is: continuing to be that exemplar of what it takes to go from being a lost soul to being full of life.

In closing, I have to add, addiction is continuing to do something in the face of mounting consequence. I was addicted to the streets and it led me to prison.

My people, while I was in the mix, I would never say this. But I'm out the mix and thinking on a sober mind, there are no pension plans for thugs. There is no 401K for gangsters. Nine times out of 10, the only guarantees are prison or the pine box. One out of ten making it to the pinnacle are not good odds...

Humbly,
Tysheem Crocker

Acknowledgments

Acknowledgments

This part of a book is about impact, importance, influence—and now I give out flowers.

First and foremost, I want to give thanks to the Lord of All the Worlds for protecting me, allowing me to grow, and for this God-given talent that has been so helpful. Even when my faith wavered, you never gave up on me. Instead, you brought me Leticia.

Leticia, my attorney, you are a godsend. You are also Momma Bear of the most important iteration of Com. v. Crocker. Everything you said you would do you have done. You said you would bring in the best, and that you did.

Alexandria Lappas, ESQ, my second lawyer on this Dream Team, you wrote the PCRA petition based on Kitty Hailey's exceptional investigation, discoveries, and Innocence Report. Brilliant writing! Thank you.

Certified Legal Investigator Kitty Hailey, I thought I knew everything about my case, until you came along. You embody the hallmark of excellence. I am so thankful for your boundless mind and impeccable investigation skills.

Nancy Mahoney, I want to thank you for your inspirational prayers and for taking notes in preparation for the investigation and eventual litigation.

Without the commitment of these women to looking out

for the little people in this rich country, proving my innocence would still be just part of my imaginative thinking.

I lost my mom, Regina Crocker, while I was serving this false imprisonment. But she was with me until her last days. Ma, I miss you dearly. Each and every day!

I must repay respect to my fosters, whom all cared for me when I couldn't care for myself: Mrs. McDonald, Gwen Hall, Pauline Paris, Larry Moss! I miss you all. Rest in peace!

Next, I would like to thank my niece Zoey. You were such a good child, and now you're a young lady headed to college. You are not just fashionably conscious; you're also gifted in academics. I've been imprisoned your entire life, yet you have allowed me to be in your life every step of the way.

My nephew Zahir, I'm glad you have carved out your own path, and it did not include the streets. Everything you want you can acquire without the help of the streets.

Special thanks to my younger bro, Shondell Crocker. Since you were able to think for yourself, you've kept me not just in your prayers, but in your life. We all we got!

Special thanks to DJ Cocoa Chanelle. While there were so many other things you could've been focused on, you took time out ya busy schedule to put my plight on a national scale, in a brilliant way too. Your philanthropy speaks volumes. Your humanity is unparalleled. Facts.

Thanks to: The Justice For Youth Foundation, WHY

Magazine, Fresh Mix Magazine, the Lady T Show, and Hassan Campbell.

My extended family—Betheas, Murrays—I miss y'all. Been too long!

Love and respect to my guy Dontaye "3" Deshields.

To my comrades, whose motives and intent were never in question, only how long we had left in each other's presence. Long after being released from prison, we remain tight. That list is very short. Brandon "King" turner, Dwayne "Dee" Watkins, and Stephen "PO" Wofford.

Stephen "PO" Wofford, when we met, I'd just hit the penitentiary yard, 21-years-young, 150 soaking wet. Even at the size, outwardly I was exuding strength, but on the inside, I was crying. Your physique was massive as was your mind.

Smooth and humble, 193 lbs., you had muscles on top of muscles, squatting 600 lbs., deadlifting 600 lbs. and benching 500 lbs.

You got me into powerlifting, helped me build my body up from puny to solid. 150 lbs. to 180 lbs. But more than that, you were my first mentor. Seeing you leave Thanksgiving 2003 was hard, but that only gave way for more growth. Here we are today, and as Kiss once said, "True to ya word, and you never lie..." I look forward to joining you in freedom.

Special shout outs to Lorenzo "Cat" Johnson and Roderick "Demon" Johnson for walking me through the exoneration process. When my mind is all over the place, I can call one of y'all. Sometimes both! Experience is the best teacher.

Special thanks to my editor, D. Utz. I told you this one is special, and you treated it like it is special.

Much love to all those who took time out their day to check on me in person while I was at my lowest: BJ. L, Robert Weisman, Casper Hill, Rab, Tiff, Mucka, Bay, Cello, Sheba, Cindy, Tisha, SaPrina, Meka, Dee, Nicole, Meek, Fay, Takia, Cassarah, Large, Chico, Baki, Shaunny, Angelique, Diamond, Shelly, Becca, Shalamar. If I missed anyone blame my mind not my heart, please.

Blessings and appreciation to all the people who purchased my books over the years. Too many to name.

Great appreciation to my contributors as I ventured into journalist mode. Brandon Key, Sam "ESQ" Ross, and Mr. Russell. I wish all three of you guys success and prosperity.

Knowledge and grinding are my two greatest gifts, (what I am best known for today), and I had lots of help with developing both. With that, I'd like to thank each and every educator and instructor who took chances by sharing their wealth in knowledge with me, fully aware that it could all go in one ear and right out the other. But, I was listening, and paying attention. Hov said it best, "you can pay for school, but you can't buy class".

I salute all those I ever grinded with — in them streets, and in the clink. Y'all know who y'all be. We don't hustle, we don't eat, we don't grind, we don't shine.

Also, big shout out to Briana Alexis; our connection is

powerful, endearing, my imagination's reward, and Lord willing it stands the test of time.

Finally, acknowledgements for my guys: My Day Ones—TankHead, Gutta, Rab, Cello, Porter, Melvin Bethune, Ern, Storm! The Bros: Lance Burke, Dennis Boney, Dame Wall, ChiTown G Garmen, Chink & Twin, Gold Mouth Geechie, Kode Red Stiffer, Mont Thomas, Don Juan, G-Baby, Seal "BN" Shuler, Knuckles, RockaFella, Dre, HR, Tee Balla, Mike Bright, Quick, Du Stutts, Akuba Prince, Rahzaq Prunty, Fly Ty, Rico, R. Gandy, Lex, Tanner Galloway, Harlem Jose, Jason Colby, Huck, Lenny, Stan Cotton, J. Franks, Almateen, Charlie R., Capone, and my guy Maurice "Mo Butta Barnes. Mo Butta, when you pulled up, you brought along a breath of fresh air!

RIP to my fallen comrades: Champ, Craig, Al Duran, Jackie. Last but not least, the big dawgs! Shannon Holmes, Wahida Clark, and Kwame "Dutch" Teague. Y'all paved a path for me to walk in. Each convo we had played a part... Facts!

Business Technology
Graduate, 2003

Made in the USA
Monee, IL
18 October 2026

66036446R00104